Downland

Anna Dillon was born in the market town of Wallingford (then Berkshire, now Oxfordshire) in 1972 and spent the first few years of her life in Wiltshire near Avebury before moving to South Oxfordshire where she still lives and works. Inspired by the ancient landscapes of the British Isles, she has been a professional artist since 2008 and has developed a vibrant signature style using bold and strong colour to reflect the form, contours and light of the land.

www.annadillon.com

Jonathan Davidson was born in Oxford in 1964, and lived in Didcot, South Oxfordshire, from 1965 until the late 1980s. He is a widely published poet and writer, with a particular interest in how poetry is heard and in how it is experienced in the natural world. He lives in the Midlands, but frequently returns to the Vale of the White Horse and the North Wessex Downs.

www.jonathandavidson.net

Also by Two Rivers Poets

David Attwooll, *The Sound Ladder* (2015)
Charles Baudelaire, *Paris Scenes* translated by
    Ian Brinton (2021)
William Bedford, *The Dancers of Colbek* (2020)
Kate Behrens, *Man with Bombe Alaska* (2016)
Kate Behrens, *Penumbra* (2019)
Kate Behrens, *Transitional Spaces* (2022)
Conor Carville, *English Martyrs* (2019)
David Cooke, *A Murmuration* (2015)
David Cooke, *Sicilian Elephants* (2021)
Tim Dooley, *Discoveries* (2022)
Jane Draycott, *Tideway* (re-issued 2022)
Jane Draycott & Lesley Saunders, *Christina
    the Astonishing* (re-issued 2022)
Claire Dyer, *The Adjustments* (2024)
Claire Dyer, *Yield* (2021)
John Froy, *The Blue Armchair* (2024)
John Froy, *Sandpaper & Seahorses* (2018)
James Harpur, *The Examined Life* (2021)
Maria Teresa Horta, *Point of Honour* translated by
    Lesley Saunders (2019)
Ian House, *Just a Moment* (2020)
Philippe Jaccottet, *In Winter Light* translated by
    Tim Dooley (2022)
Rosie Jackson, *Love Leans over the Table* (2023)
Rosie Jackson & Graham Burchell, *Two Girls and a Beehive:
    Poems about Stanley Spencer and Hilda Carline* (2020)
Martha Kapos, *Music, Awake Her* (2024)
Gill Learner, *Chill Factor* (2016)
Gill Learner, *Change* (2021)
Sue Leigh, *Chosen Hill* (2018)
Sue Leigh, *Her Orchards* (2021)
Becci Louise, *Octopus Medicine* (2017)
Mairi MacInnes, *Amazing Memories of Childhood, etc.* (2016)
Steven Matthews, *On Magnetism* (2017)
Steven Matthews, *Some Other Where* (2023)
Henri Michaux, *Storms under the Skin* translated by
    Jane Draycott (2017)
Kate Noakes, *Goldhawk Road* (2023)

René Noyau, *Earth on Fire and other Poems* translated by
    Gérard Noyau with Peter Pegnall (2021)
James Peake, *Reaction Time of Glass* (2019)
James Peake, *The Star in the Branches* (2022)
Vic Pickup (ed), *Reading Poets: A new anthology* (2024)
David Ricks, *With Signs Following* (2024)
Peter Robinson & David Inshaw, *Bonjour Mr Inshaw* (2020)
Peter Robinson, *English Nettles* (re-issued 2022)
Peter Robinson, *Retrieved Attachments* (2023)
Lesley Saunders, *Nominy-Dominy* (2018)
Lesley Saunders, *This Thing of Blood & Love* (2022)
Jack Thacker, *Handling* (2018)
Robin Thomas, *The Weather on the Moon* (2022)
Susan Utting, *The Colour of Rain* (2024)
Jean Watkins, *Precarious Lives* (2018)

Downland

Paintings by Anna Dillon

Poems by Jonathan Davidson

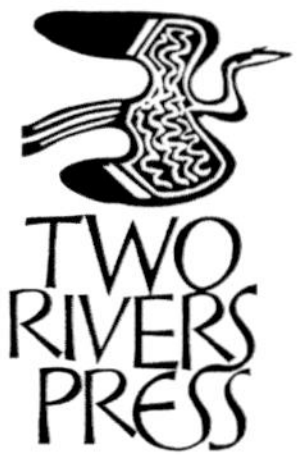

First published in the UK in 2024 by Two Rivers Press
7 Denmark Road, Reading RG1 5PA
www.tworiverspress.com

ISBN 978-1-915048-12-7

1 2 3 4 5 6 7 8 9

Two Rivers Press is represented in the UK by Inpress Ltd and distributed by BookSource.

Cover painting: *The Icknield Way* (2016) by Anna Dillon. Oil on board, 605 mm × 720 mm.

Cover design by Nadja Robinson
Text design by Nadja Robinson and typeset in Parisine and Janson
Map design by Nadja Robinson and Sally Castle

Printed and bound in Great Britain by Halstan & Co., Amersham

Contents

Acknowledgements

Subscribers

Anna Dillon, Jonathan Davidson and Two Rivers Press are grateful to the following subscribers for their support for this publication:

Abigail Campbell	Gregory Leadbetter	Philip Rush
Alison Brackenbury	Harriett Cleaver	Qaisra Shahraz MBE
Amanda Smyth	Heather Wilson	Regina Weinert
Amelia Dowler	James Caruth	Rita Walker
Andrew Hoaen	Jane Commane	Rob Foster
Andy Croft	Jane Morland	Rod Whitworth
Ann Jay	Jeff Phelps	Roger Voller
Anne Caldwell	Jeremy Platt	Rosie Boulton
Bean Sawyer	Jo and Pat Walshe	Roy and Trish Walker
Bert Flitcroft	Jo Bell	Roz Goddard
Brenda Read-Brown	John Hedge	Ruth Higgins
Caroline Shaw	Jonathan Coleclough	Sally Goldsmith
Chris Kinsey	Judith Allnatt	Sally Reynolds,
Clare Brown	Lesley Curwen	remembering Beryl & Roy
David Clarke	Lisa Peter	Sam Henley Smith
David Harmer	Liz England	Sam Ward
Deborah Alma	Lydia Harris	Sandra van Lente
Deborah Catesby	Maura Dooley	Scott Clark
Derek Littlewood	Michael Blackburn	Shantel Edwards
Derek Neale	Nigel Pantling	Simon Thirsk
Derek Nisbet	Patrick and Gemma	Stella Thebridge
Di Slaney	Malaperiman	Stewart Sanderson
Estelle Price	Paul Kavanagh	Stuart Bartholomew
Gail Webb	Paul McDonald	Susan Alexander
Gary Carr	Peter Foster	Susannah Chisholm
Gary McKeone	Peter Walker	Suzanne Conway
Gladstone's Library	Philip Binding	Suzanne Iuppa

Sylvia Davidson   Tim Daw   Wendy Klein
Tess and Paul Isherwood   Tim Dee   William Gallagher
The Poetic Licence   Tony Ruane   Yvonne Hyde

Thanks

I would like to thank my husband, Guy Liverton, who enabled me to take
the uncertain step towards becoming a professional landscape artist.
Without his support I would never have been able to achieve my lifetime
ambition to paint for the rest of my life. I would also like to extend my
thanks to all my family and friends who have supported me.
— Anna Dillon

My thanks to the many friends who have read and commentated on
various versions of these poems, including members of *The Zellig Poetry
Group* (particularly to Liz Berry, Emma Purshouse, Jane Commane,
Gregory Leadbetter) and to other poetry friends, including Roz Goddard.
   I am indebted to Peter Sansom, who reads and hears my work like no-one
else. My thanks to the many people who have walked the Ridgeway with
 me, sharing poems and wonder, and especially to Lisa Peter.
— Jonathan Davidson

Our thanks to Peter, Anne, Sally and Nadja at Two Rivers Press for their
magnificent work on this book.
— Anna Dillon & Jonathan Davidson

Introduction

'Those only know a country who are acquainted with its footpaths. By the roads, indeed, the outside may be seen; but the footpaths go through the heart of the land.'
— Richard Jefferies, *The Amateur Poacher*, 1879

Ridgeways were ancient tracks that ran along the spine of hills, a more reliable way of travelling than having to negotiate forested valleys, flood plains, bogs and rivers. These paths were the favoured route of drovers and soldiers. After the enclosure acts of the mid-18th century, one of these several ancient paths, the Ridgeway, as we know it now, became more clearly defined and since the 1970s, it has become a National Trail, stretching more than 80 miles from Wiltshire to Buckinghamshire. It passes through two Areas of Outstanding Natural Beauty, the Chilterns, to the east of the Thames, and the North Wessex Downs to the west. The Ridgeway remains a green path where anyone can step out and walk in the footsteps of the earliest settlers and visitors to this island. It sometimes becomes one with the Icknield Way. The latter is a lower path which at times skirts the foothills, at times joins the road. There is an Upper Icknield Way and a Lower Icknield Way and much discussion as to where they start and finish. The poet, Edward Thomas, was unable to solve this continuing debate of where and how and saw in that fact something of the very essence of these landscapes:

> I could not find a beginning or an end of the Icknield Way. It is thus a symbol of mortal things with their beginnings and ends always in immortal darkness. (*The Icknield Way*, 1913)

Ancient barrows, mounds and earthworks line these routes, and sarsen stones are scattered singly and in groups along their length. These are mankind's interventions, a fact which sometimes distracts from, as well as enhances and interestingly complicates, the simple beauty of the land itself. W. G. Hoskins in *The Making of the English Landscape* (1955), writes, 'Not much of England, even in its more withdrawn, inhuman places, has escaped being altered by man in some subtle way or other, however untouched we fancy it is at first sight.' The influence of this particular book on Jonathan Davidson's feeling for landscape, industry, history and class is clear. He tells us in 'Juniper Hollow', of his fourth reading of it and how Hoskins himself, 'read the landscape like a book'.

This combination of nature, history, folklore, geography, politics and mystery provides a potent source for two lively minds fortunate enough to have grown up in this landscape. Anna Dillon and Jonathan Davidson are newest in a long line of artists and writers to respond.

From Eric Ravilious, Paul Nash, Stanley Spencer and John Piper to Fay Godwin's photographs, artists have been drawn to this topography. In Spencer Gore's vibrant Modernist view of the Icknield Way and Brian Cook's striking covers for the mid-century Batsford Guides, we can see the precursors to Dillon's vivid, jewelled depictions of light, earth and seasonal variation.

Kenneth Grahame, John Betjeman, Thomas Hughes, and a line down from George Borrow through William Morris, leads to perhaps one of the best-known interpreters of this landscape, the poet Edward Thomas, who published his account of walking the Icknield Way in 1913. Thomas was interested in ancient roads, inspired by Hilaire Belloc's *Old Road*, and drawn too by the writings of Richard Jefferies. More recently, calling Thomas his 'guiding spirit', nature writer Robert MacFarlane began his book about the ancient paths, *The Old Ways*, by walking the Icknield Way, and Thomas's biographer the poet Matthew Holllis and the playwright Nick Dear both retraced his steps in forging new work of their own. Yet in considering the tradition of painting or writing about these landscapes, I have never been more conscious of the material absence of women. Where are the hidden feet and hands that laboured, the imaginations which gave birth to and fostered the flights of others? Where are the contributions which might form our own line of inheritance? For as Jonathan Davidson tells us, 'Lines are what we live by' ('Towards Uffington'). How welcome then is Anna Dillon's evocative and dazzling interpretation of these extraordinary landscapes. Her attention to form and contour and her audacious palette speak as clearly and precisely as Davidson's attentive verse.

These are landscapes that in literary terms suggest a person walking alone and in silent contemplation, yet Edward Thomas's *The Icknield Way* (1913) is an account of walks taken often in the company of his brother Julian, and Robert MacFarlane regularly walks with his friend Johnny Flynn. Such collaborations can be powerful. Think of John Piper's work with John Betjeman on the Shell Guides, and Robert MacFarlane's work with Jackie Morris. W. G. Hoskins worked with the photographer Frederick Attenborough (father of David Attenborough) all down the years. The sympathy and understanding between them enriching their work as a whole. What a sensitive and perceptive partnership Davidson and Dillon have made, each artist reveals something of themselves but by working together the effect is to illuminate, never merely to illustrate.

Davidson's cycle of poems (was there ever a more apt term for a sequence of works that begins and ends on bicycles) is both a memoir told through a series of moments in a landscape and a meditation on time. He wears lightly his deep knowledge of the geology, history, industry of the region and from the very first poem ('In the Beginning – Two Cyclists') in which father and son find 'a watch still ticking', takes the reader with him as fellow traveller ('Sparsholt Down'):

> We're all of us there –
> related and unrelated –
> crossing the landscape,

As Wordsworth advised, he writes after he has 'thought long and deeply' and his is 'emotion recollected in tranquility'. For the cast that walks with Davidson are all long gone, from the family of father and mother to the families we create through friendship, work and familiarity, from a remembrance of fellow poet David Hart to the 'fat, sad souls of cooling towers' ('The Industrial Henge'). Just as Dillon's paintings do not include a single person or dwelling, so Davidson writes, 'Everything that was is not'.

Like Davidson, Thomas Hardy often took his bicycle out into the countryside and it is possible that his poem 'The Shadow on the Stone', may have its origin in a cycle ride along the Ridgeway. Written in grief after the death of his wife Emma, he thinks he senses her while out walking, 'I thought her behind my back'. The experience evokes a haunting that is both welcome and uneasy for the poet:

> So I went on softly from the glade,
> And left her behind me throwing her shade,
> As she were indeed an apparition —
> My head unturned lest my dream should fade.

Hardy knows that to hold onto this precious moment he must not look back, as Orpheus once did, only to find it was a dream. In the same way Davidson shows us, time and again in these poems, that all of us live on in each other's memories for as long as our hearts, like the watch he finds in the opening poem, continue to tick, and we are all together 'when the last wheel has buckled' hidden though we may be,

> … in the field of wheat
> or else in the beautiful autumnal,
> metallic clump of beech trees on the hill.

Davidson's final poem sees 'two cyclists', who may or may not be the father and son cyclists of the opening poem, disappear into the land itself, together in the knowledge that in the end we all return to dust.

Maura Dooley

For my late mother,
who gave me poetry and stories,

and my late father,
who gave me cycling and politics.

— Jonathan Davidson

In the Beginning – Two Cyclists

My Dad and I
used to ride out south
cycling with the Cycling Club
on Sundays or on our own.

We often found rabbits
and sometimes pigeons
and great black blackberries.
One year we found strawberries.

Once we found a watch still ticking.

Lammy Down

I see where I must go,
always heading home:

the beech hanger, the
bleach-boned horse,

green ringing smithy,
six lost towers, spring-

line villages watching
as I lope across a low

horizon; my shadow
stretched out ahead.

The 'six lost towers' are of Didcot Power Station. Built in 1970,
it was demolished – and partially collapsed with tragic results
– between 2014 and 2020.

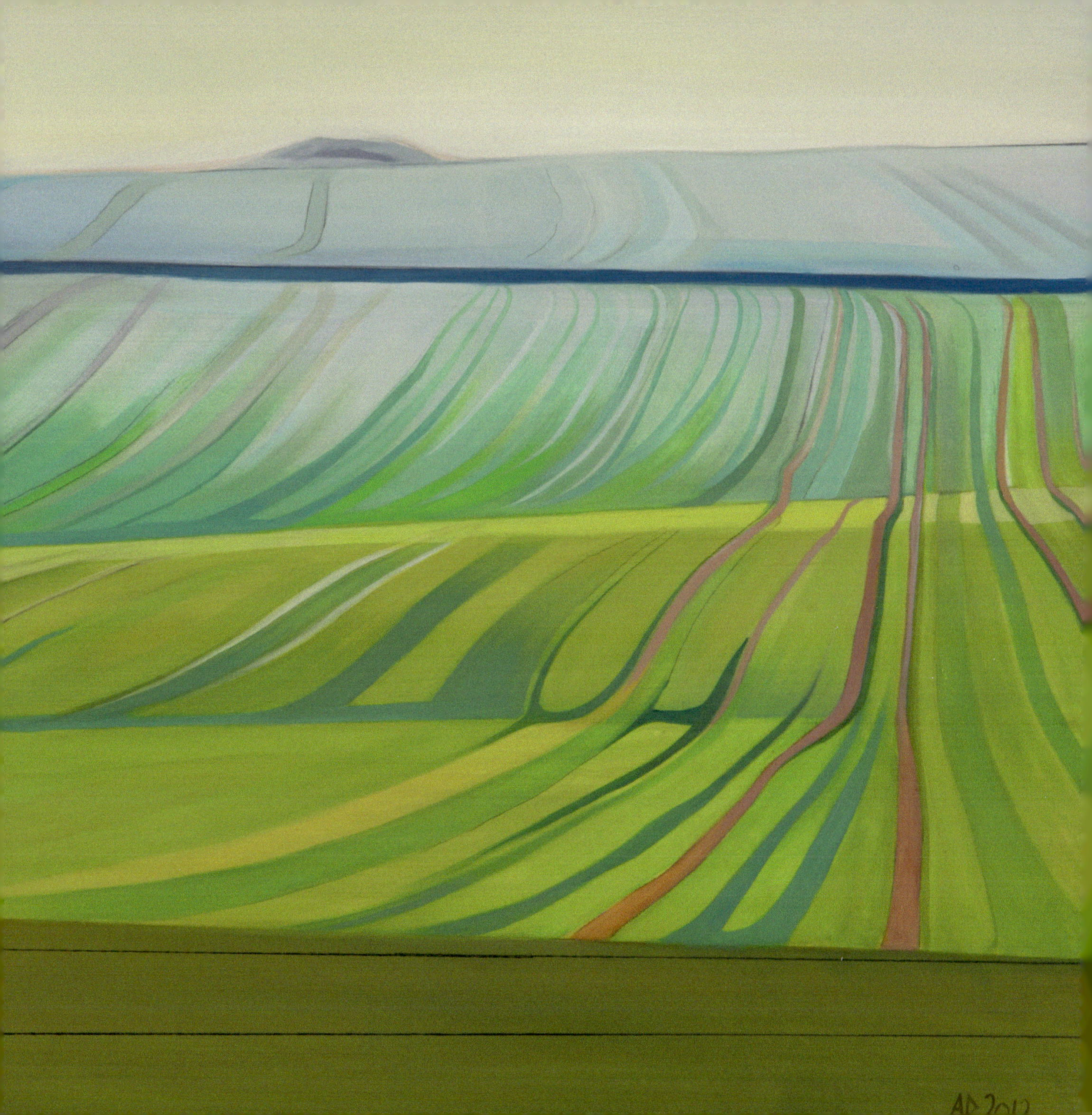
AD 2012

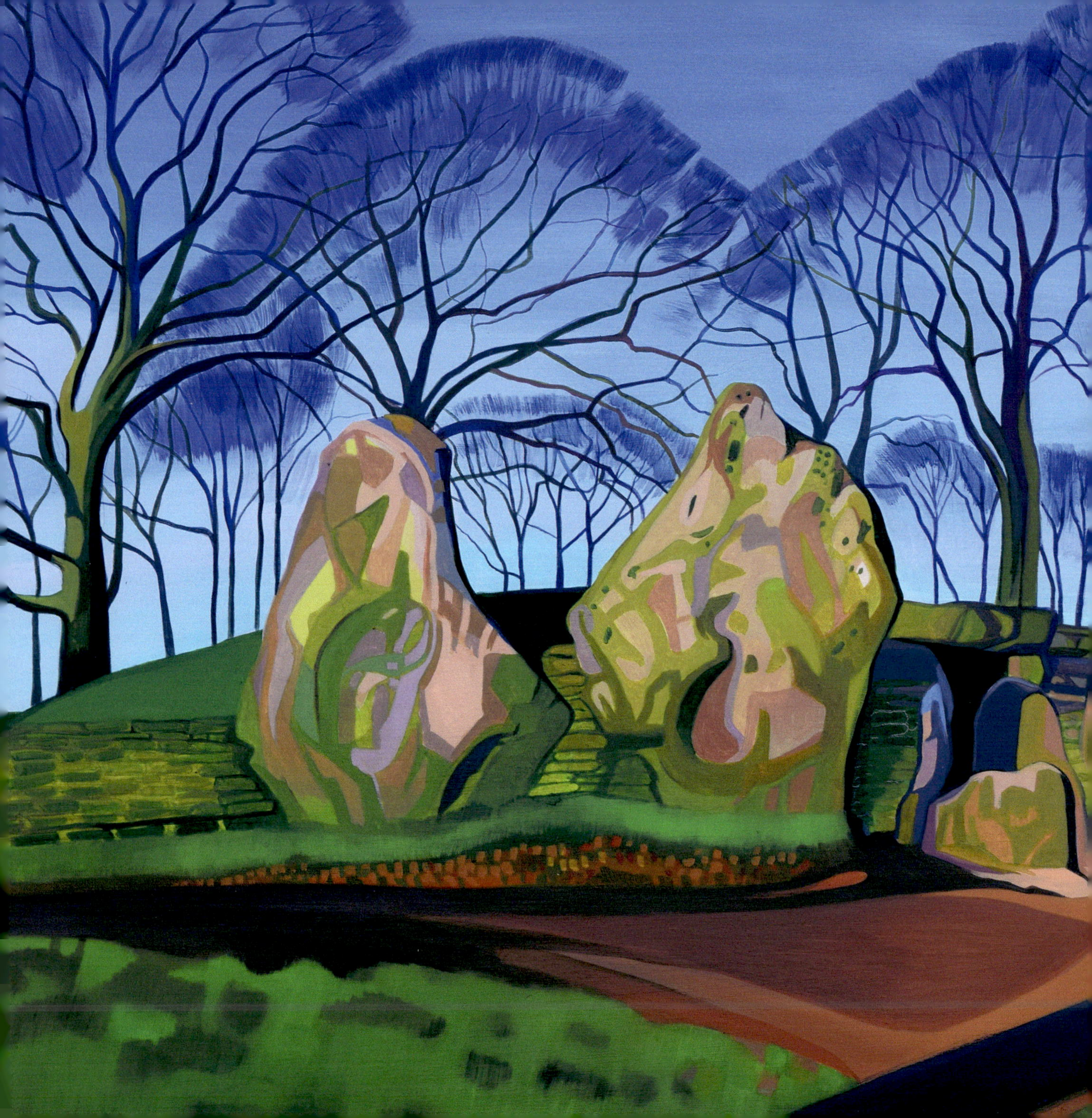

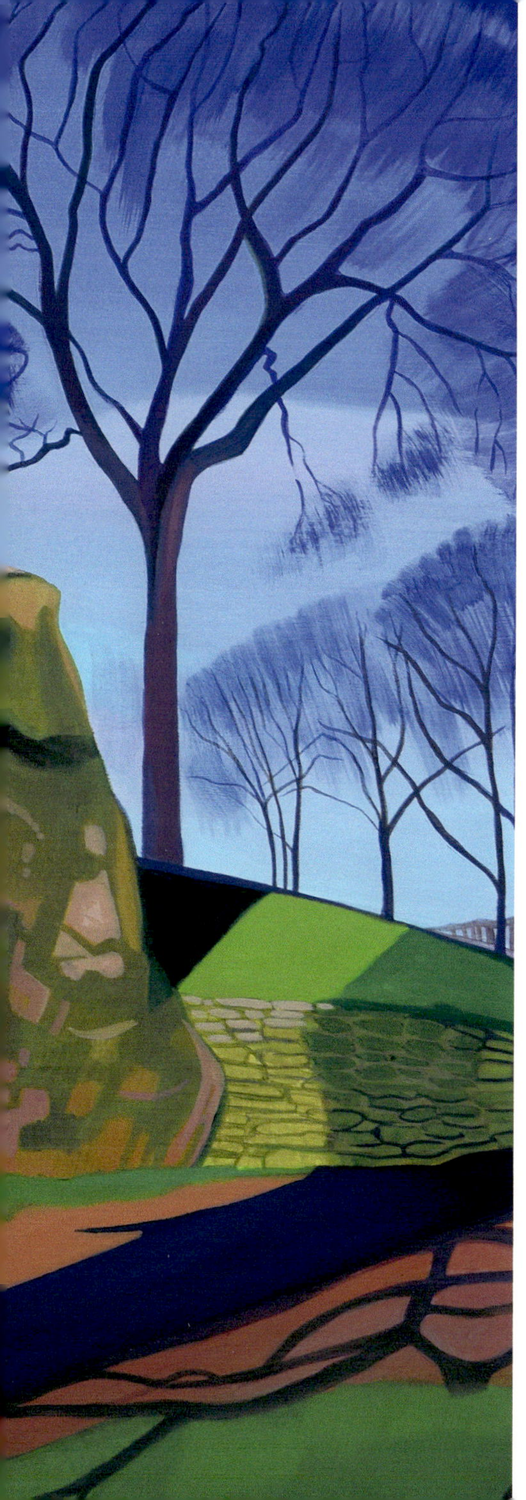

Wayland's Smithy

This clear morning, cold rolls up
from the vale. The rooks circle
a little to the south. When I go
they'll come back, black rags
throwing themselves in the air.

I stand myself before the stones
staring them into stillness. I know
that, when I go, they'll lean down
towards each other, conferring,
concluding that I'm harmless.

For the moment, they don't move.
Then the time shifts slightly, some
others join me. One takes my hand
and walks me down into the dark,
back to the beginning and the end.

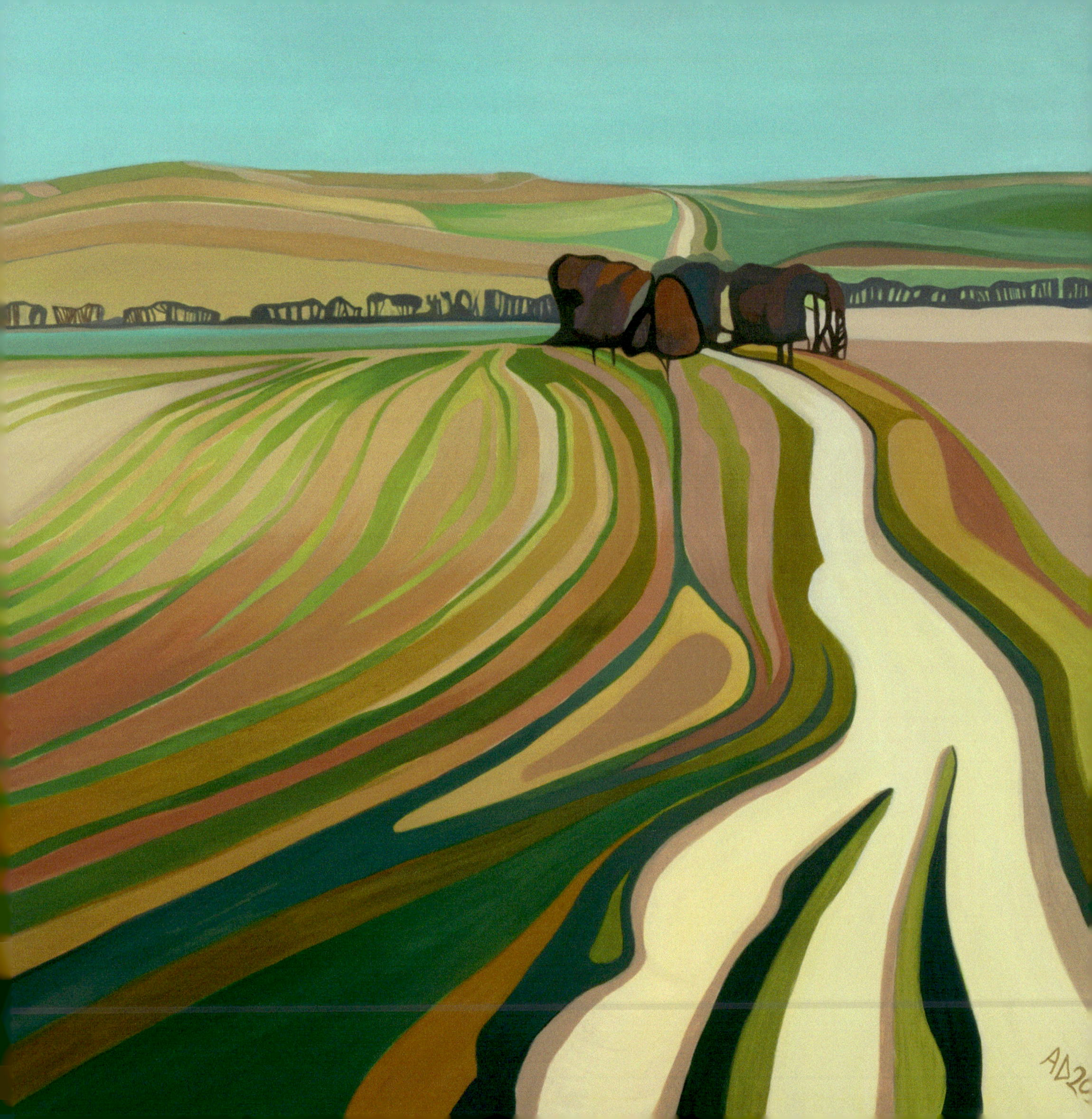

Towards Uffington

Pulled tight, the country ripples
like cloth;
released, the fields fall back
into shape,
Towards Uffington.

We haul the ropes that change
the landscape;
say our words and sing
our song,
Towards Uffington.

Lines are what we live by,
fading lines;
they tighten time then suddenly
go slack,
And down we go.

Frost on the Manger

A cold corner of the sweeping down.
A thousand-year frost
on ice-gelled quiffs of tussocks,
and every seed head held still.

A little road flows to the vale,
the sun-lit lowlands,
our inland ocean, our new Pacific;
and every wave is wheat or barley.

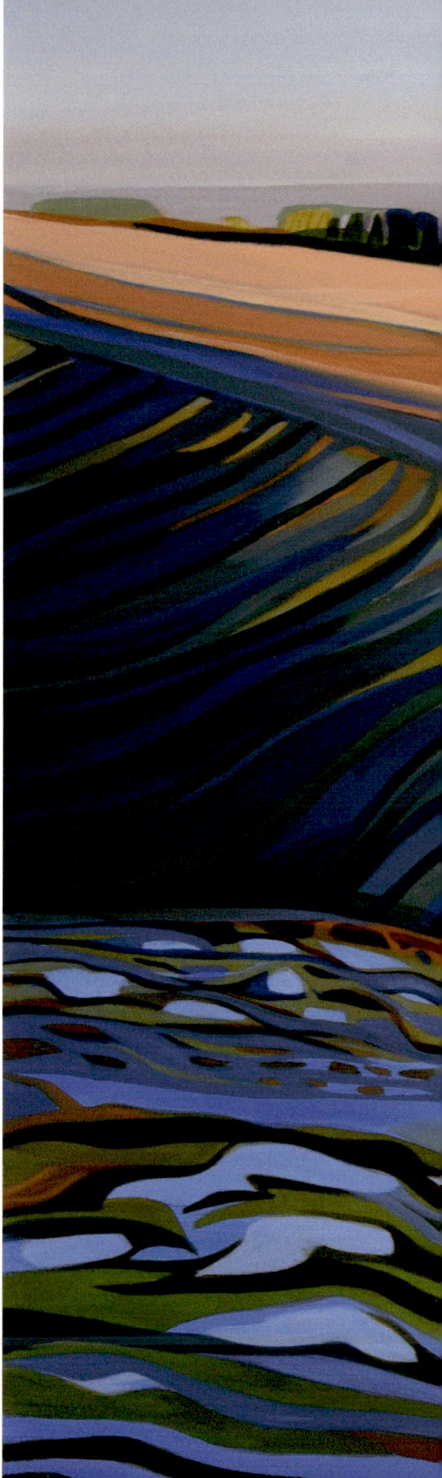

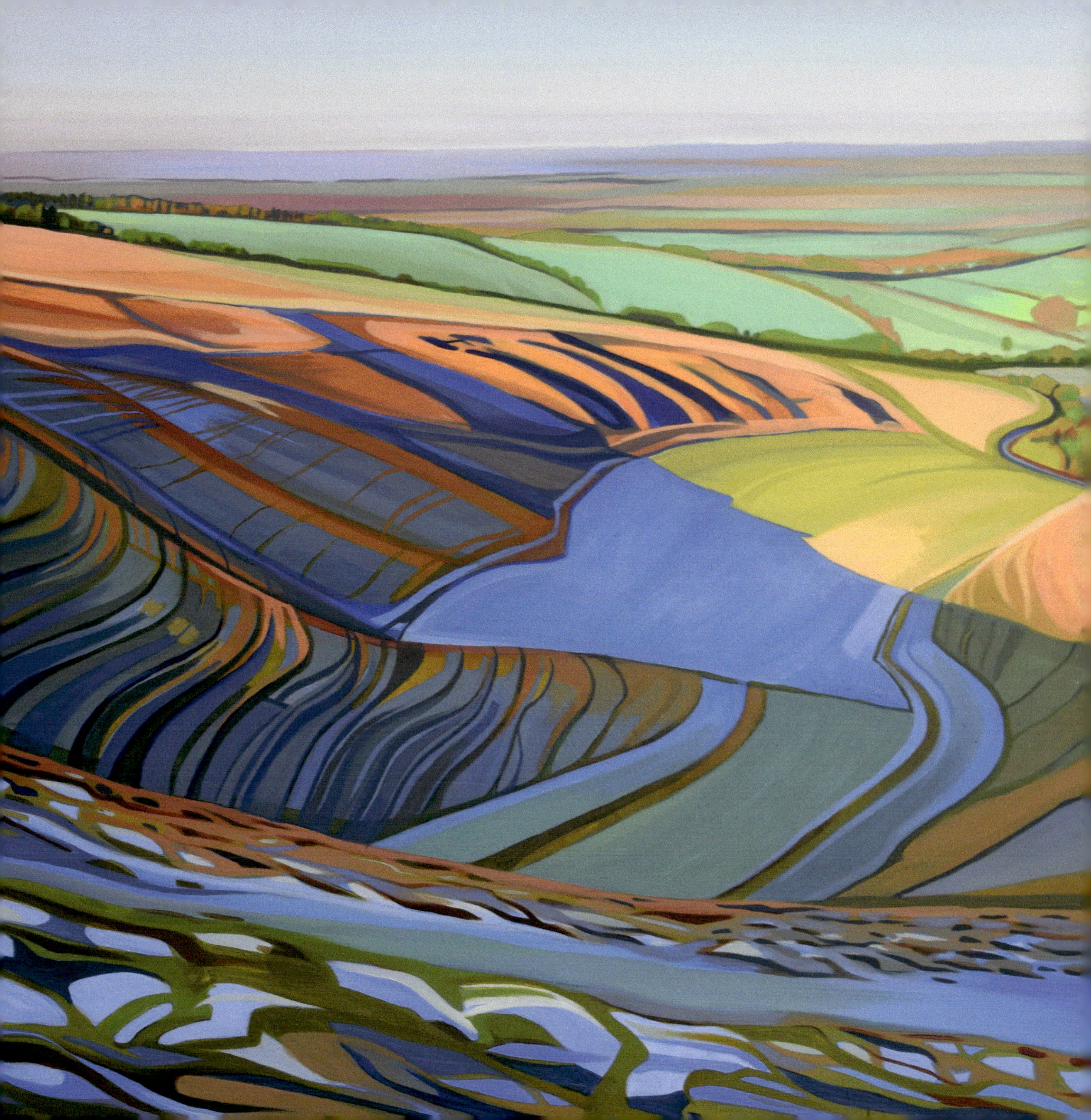

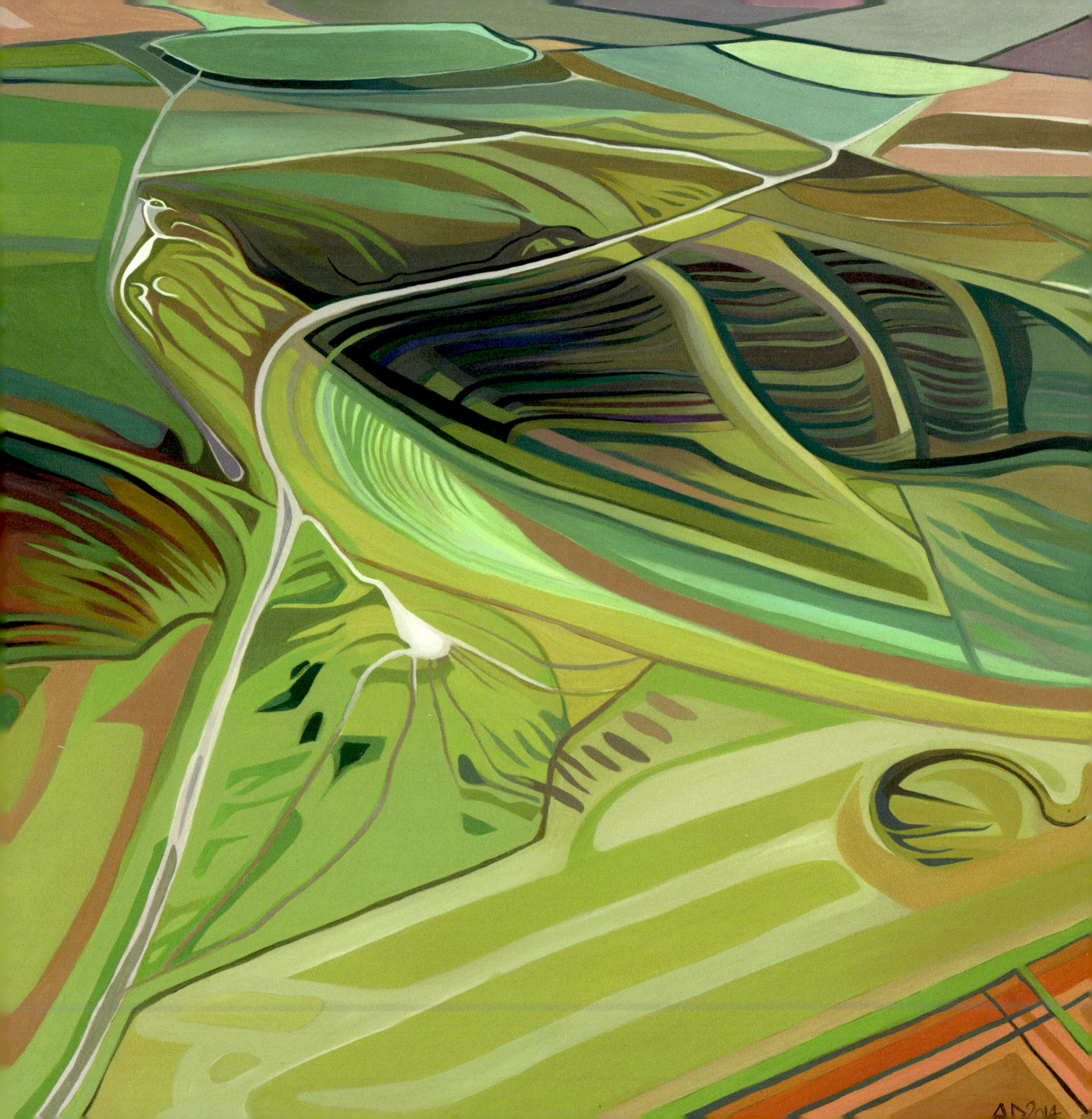

The Aerial Horse

Anna, you are so bold to use orange
and purple, corroded copper, golden
pink. I see simply green or brown.

Only the bare horse is anywhere
near white, which as we know is
all or nothing. So, paint, like words,

needs emptiness, a shouting silence
to tip the colour into. Now, the earth
looks up, fixing us with that one eye.

Rams Hill Coombe

Thunder forecast,
even the pelts
of roadkill bristle.

Land bends, buckles
under cloud weight.
Vast shadows shift

slowly into place.
Under bare trees
beech mast lifts un–

settled, then settles.
We wait for rain.

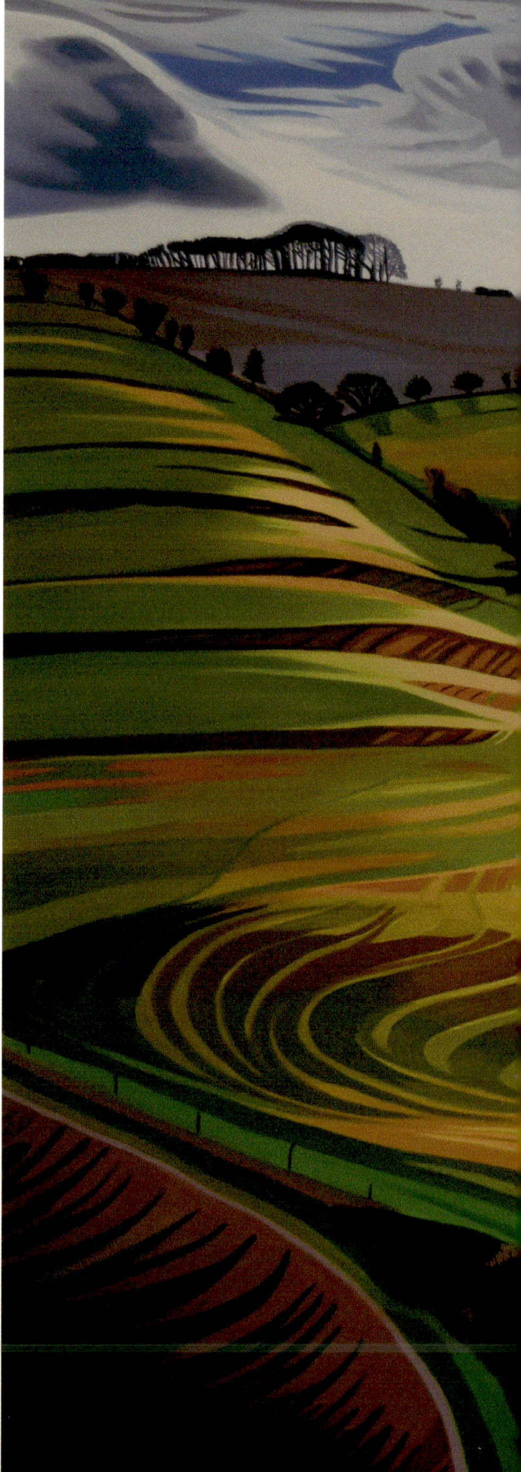

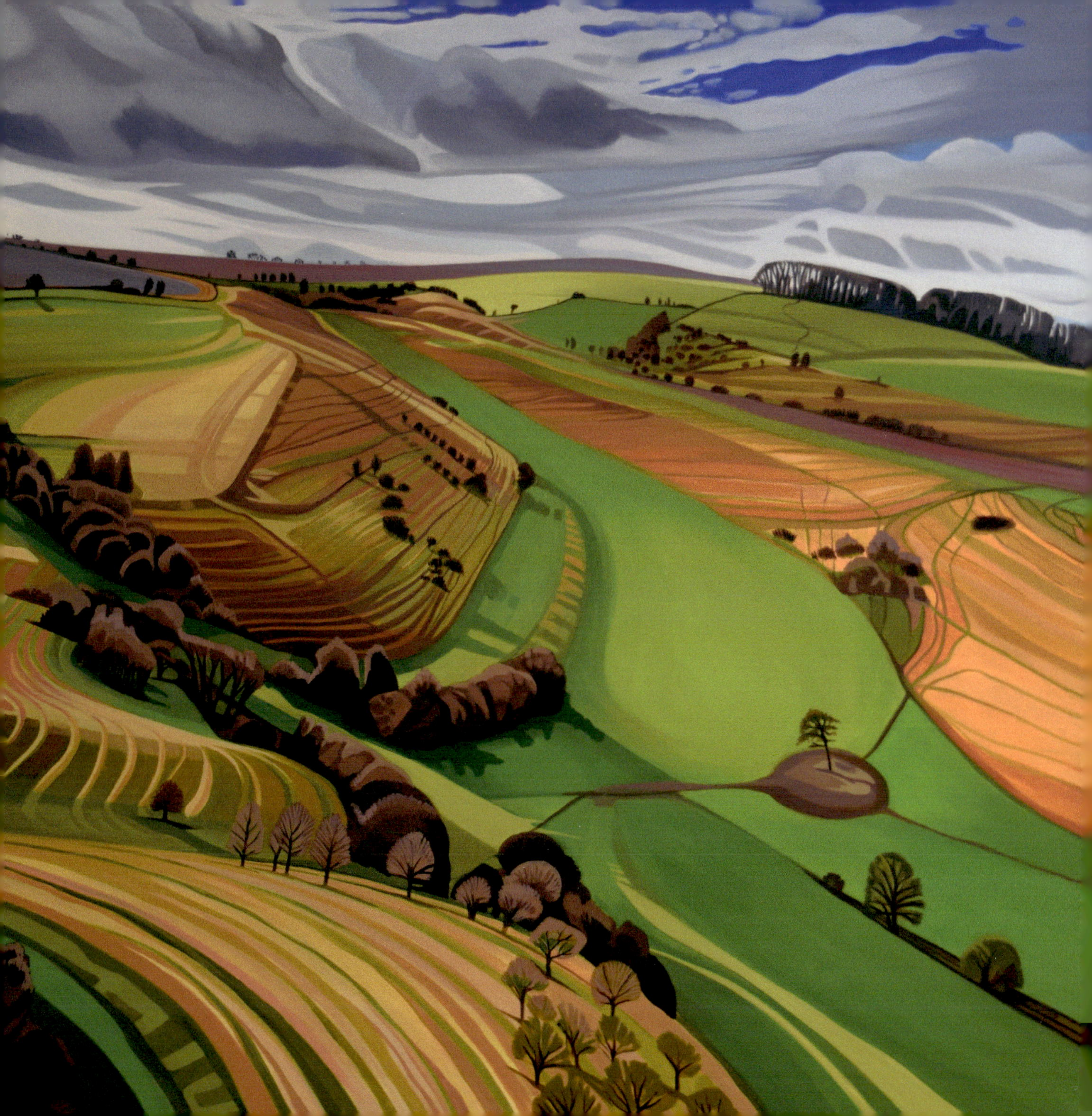

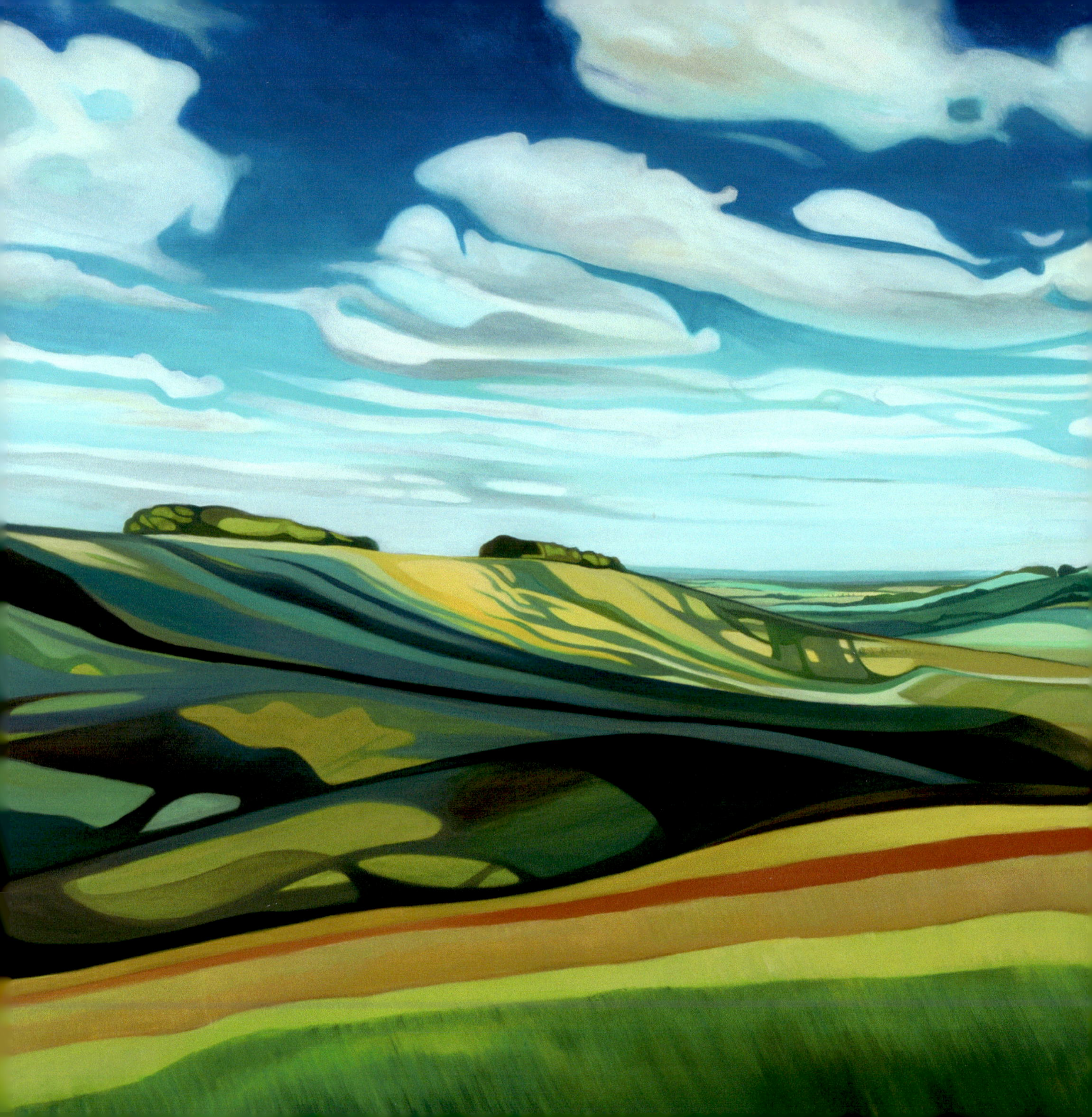

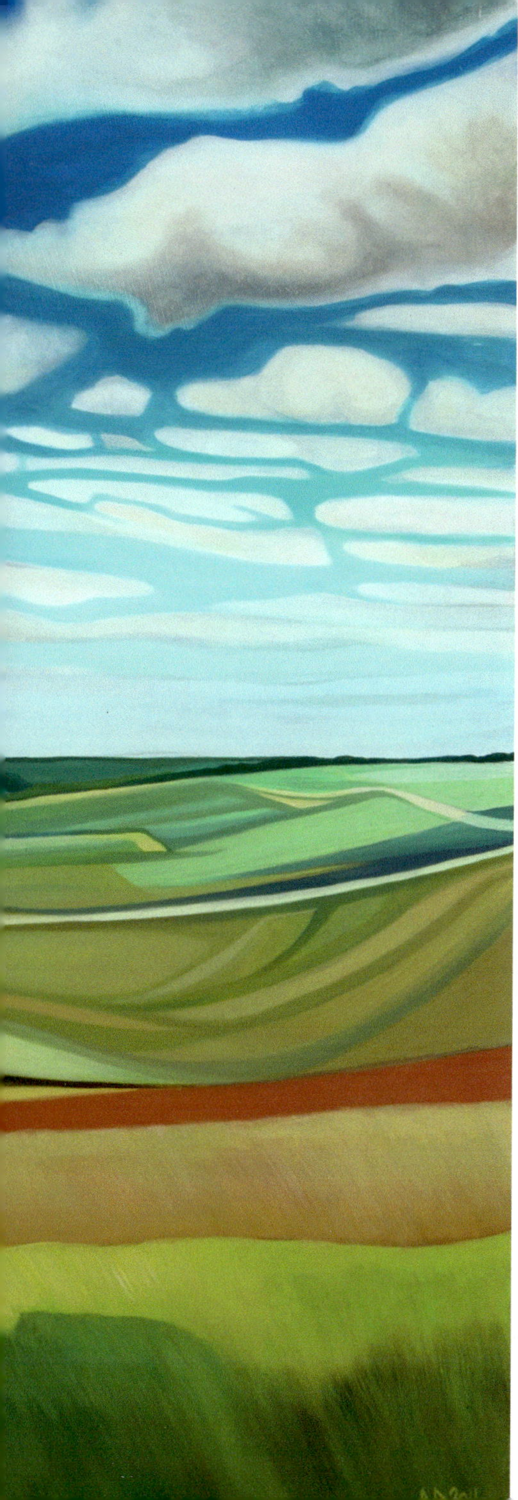

The Devil's Delight

From my rowing boat
I trail a hand
into the cloudy waters,
unknowingly deep.

Then, I look up *onto*
the thunderous patchwork
of vapour, caught in its
greens and yellows.

Shortly, the rain will collapse,
many small bullet holes will open
in the blue and white water.

The heaven of earth
will empty itself
into the sea of air.

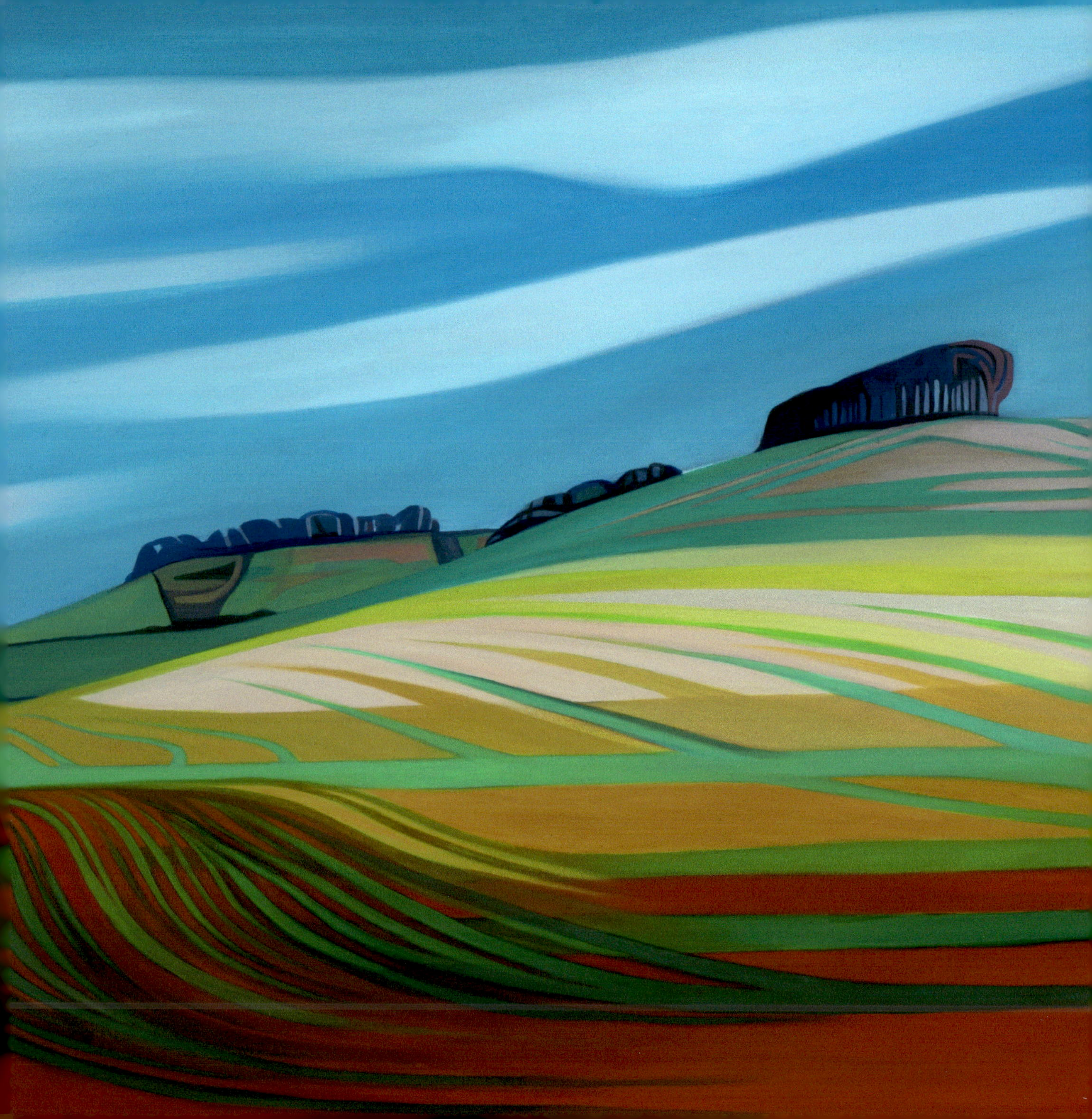

Sparsholt Down

Not a bad day to be out
in the open: the hill ahead,
the traditional trees.

Walker walking beneath
the extraordinary blue,
simply keep walking –

you are there somewhere,
found among field paths
or entering the trees.

We're all of us there –
related and unrelated –
crossing the landscape,

our dead lives lacing
the field net of the living,
whatever ways we went.

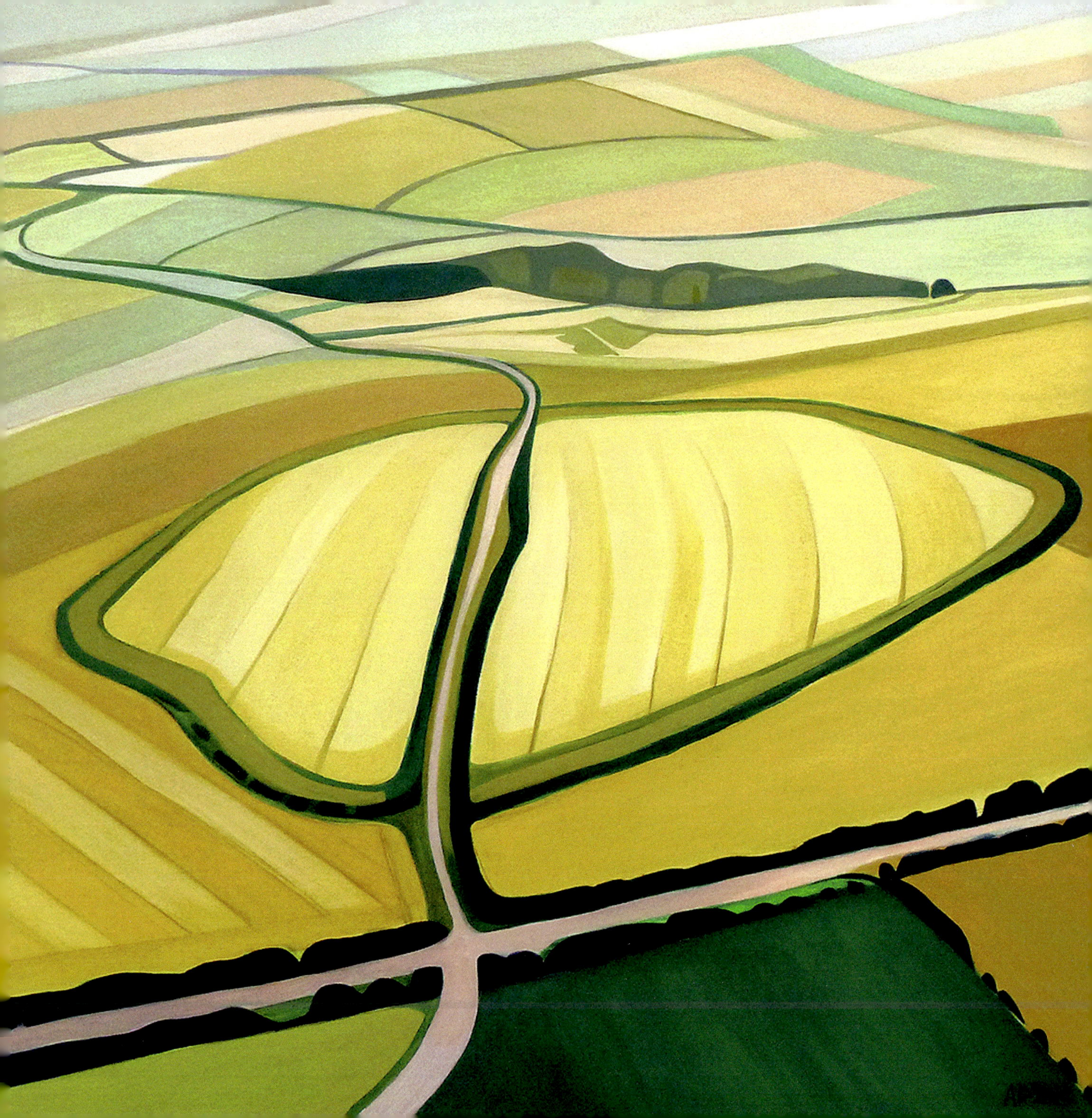

Segsbury Camp

Riding my bicycle of thought along
now dusty ways, adjacent and within
Segsbury Camp, I am suddenly struck

by a small stone dropped or more likely
thrown by a crow who has inexplicably
taken against me and my bicycle.

Oh, crow, are *you* able to ride a bike –
of thought or otherwise – around and about
the environs of Segsbury Camp? No,

I thought not.

Farnborough View

Well, everything is underground,
of course, soundless or unheard.

Here, things are unspoken, not
without power but without the need

to exert it. Certainly, there will be
dark waters, an aquifer, a lost

lake lapping at rushed margins –
extreme, extensive, calcium scarring –

a great space opening up below;
not faith or hope or hopelessness

or a metaphor for hopelessness,
but a useful submerged pond.

The aquifer in the Thames Basin supplies drinking water
and supports river-flows through many chalk streams.

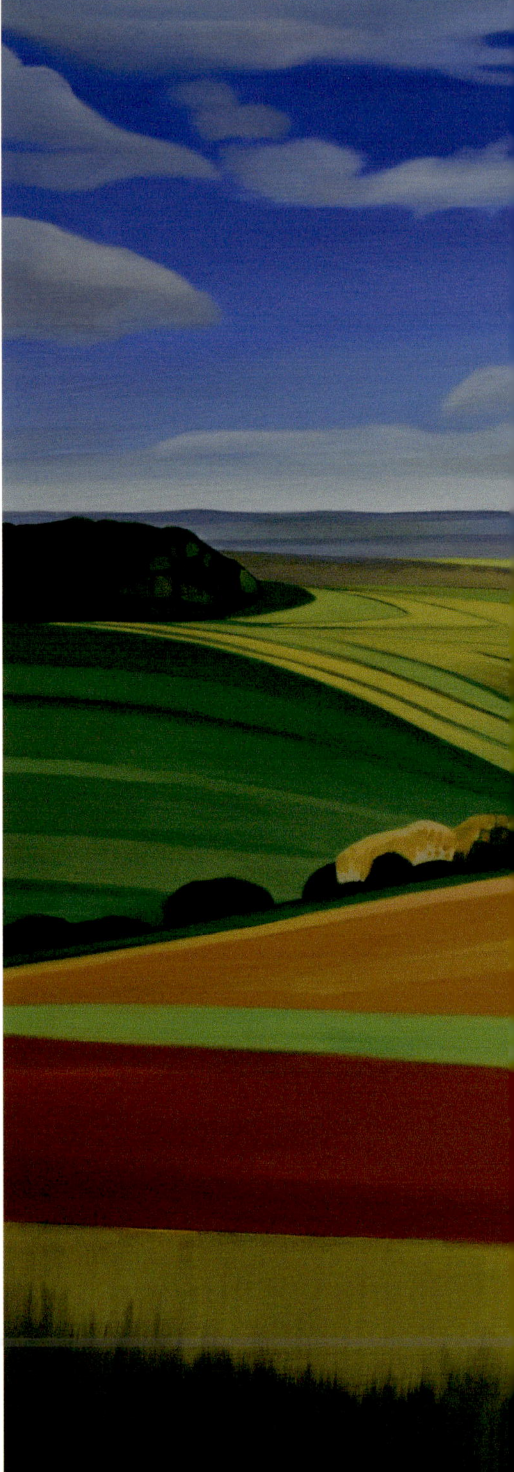

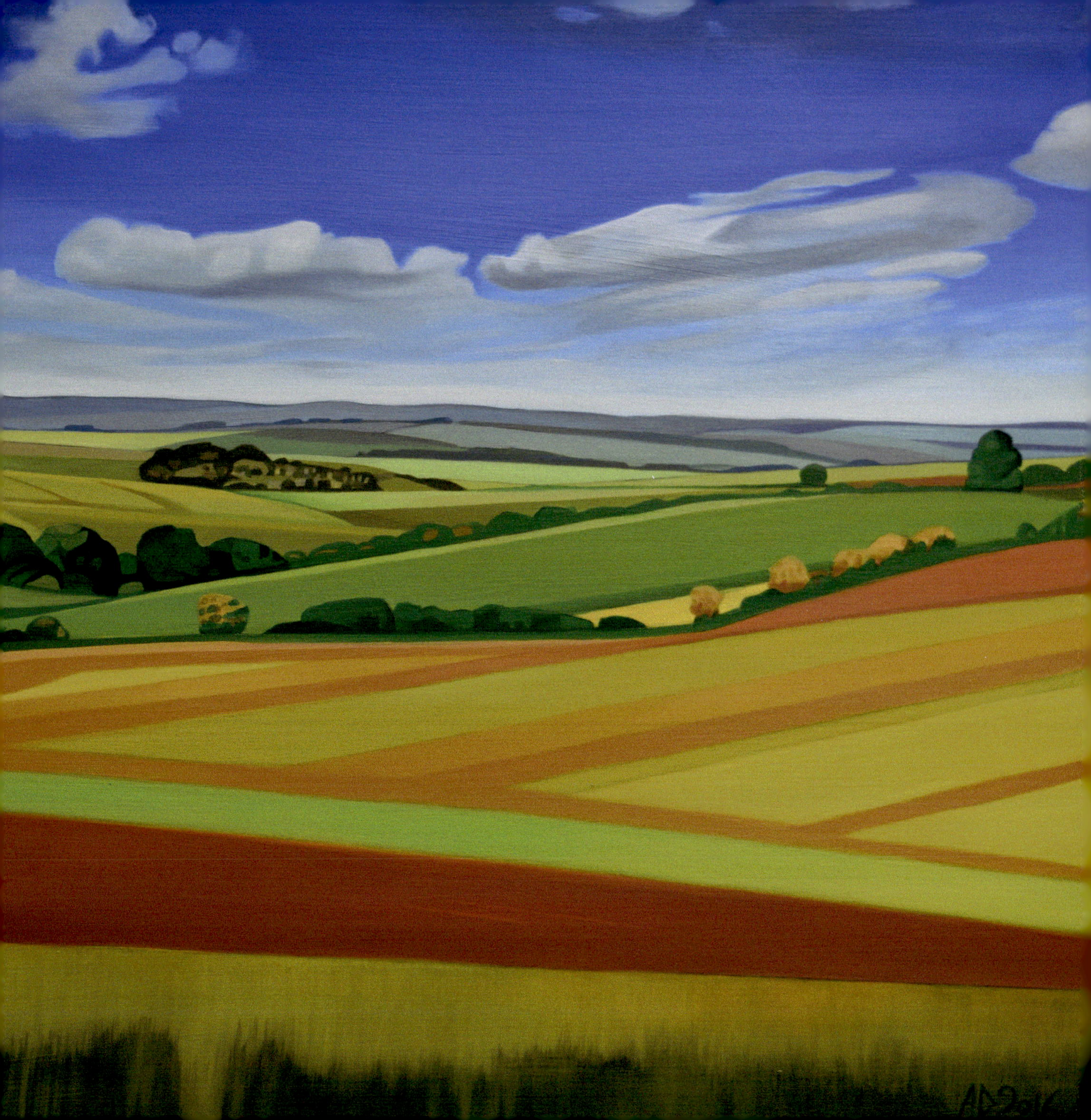

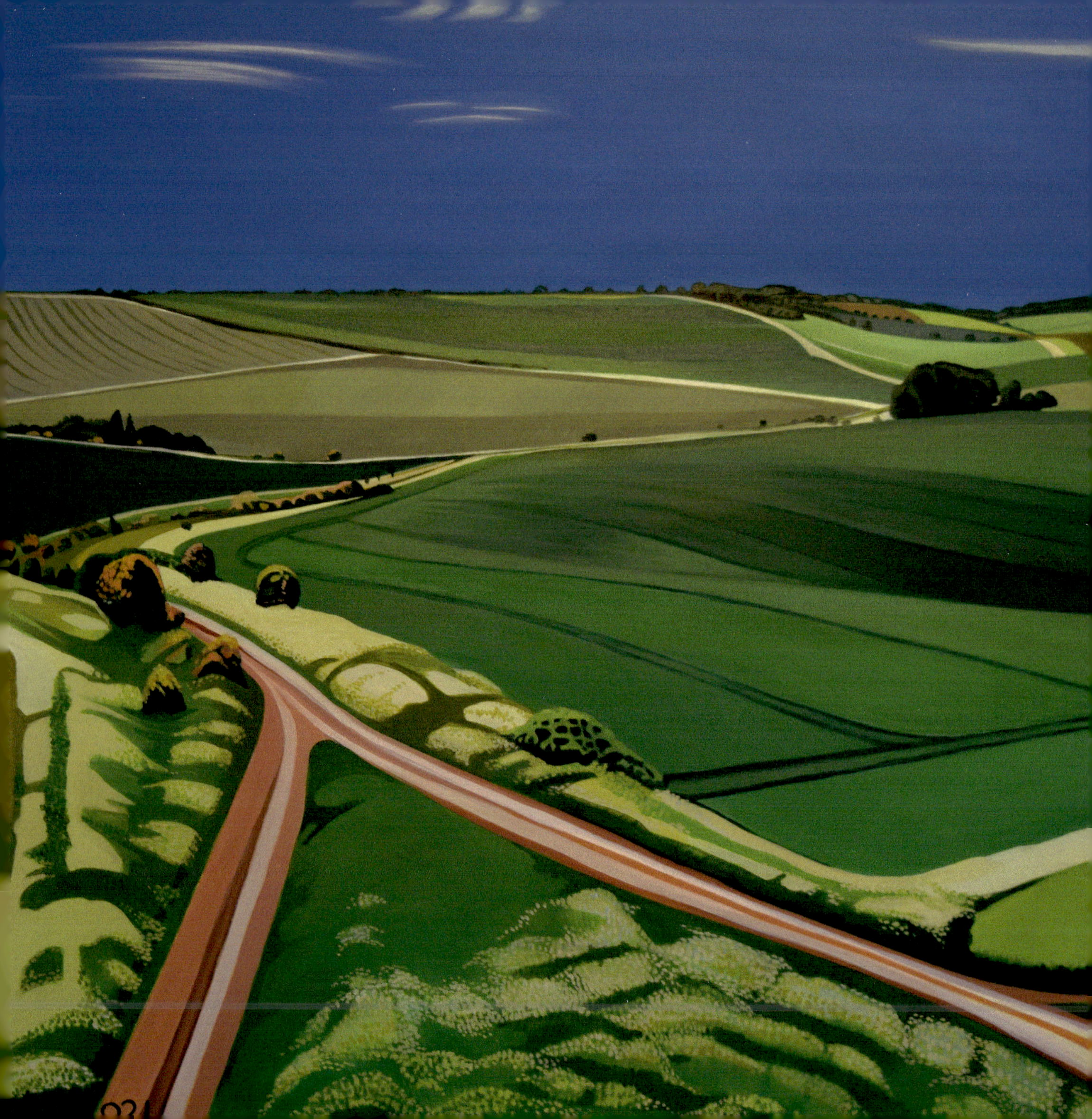

Old Down

Write me a line like a lane
or track or bridleway,
coming down off Old Down
to loam or greensand
or clay.

Speak me a line like a lane
where white has soured to grey –
rain-soaked rut-puddled path
down-headed, plodding
away.

Or...

Sing me a line like a lane
that drifts the upper way –
worn well, flint-nailed drove road
with a drover's swagger
and sway.

Bury Down

i.m. Roy Frederick Davidson

We stood for two hundred years to hear
the coming of the railway, to hear
the arrival of the dual carriageway,

to see war planes enclosing the sky,
into which now you are carefully thrown,
un-animated, cold blooded, gone for good.

Dad, what's left of you is flown, dark dust
lifted into thin air, a man released from all
his days, and away, and away, and away.

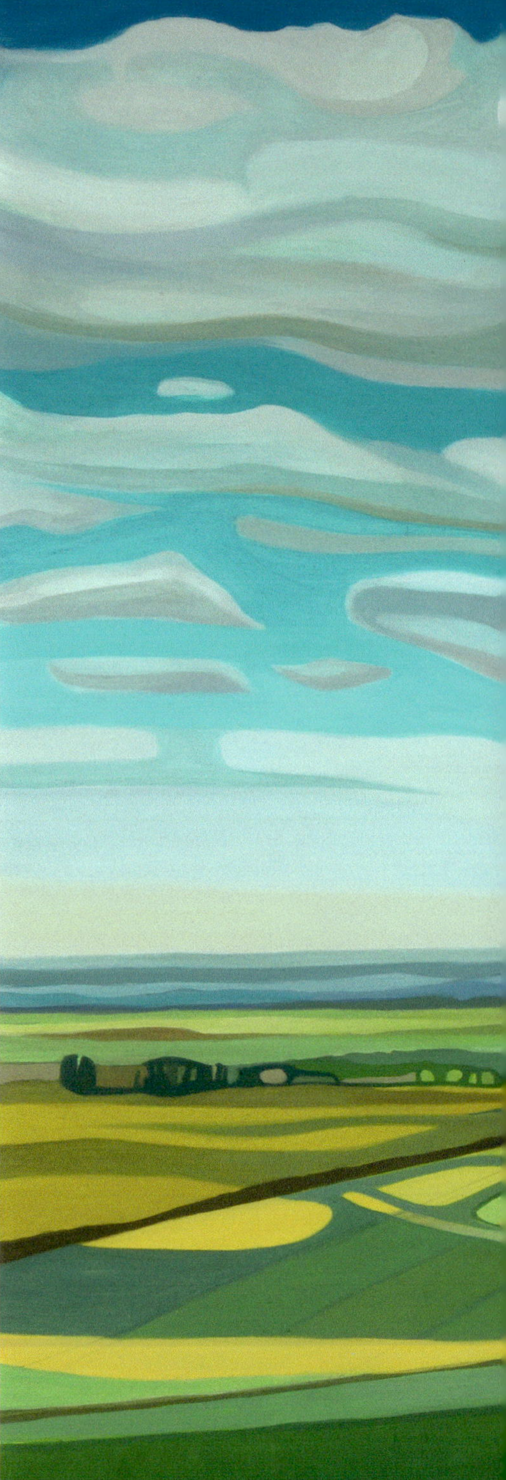

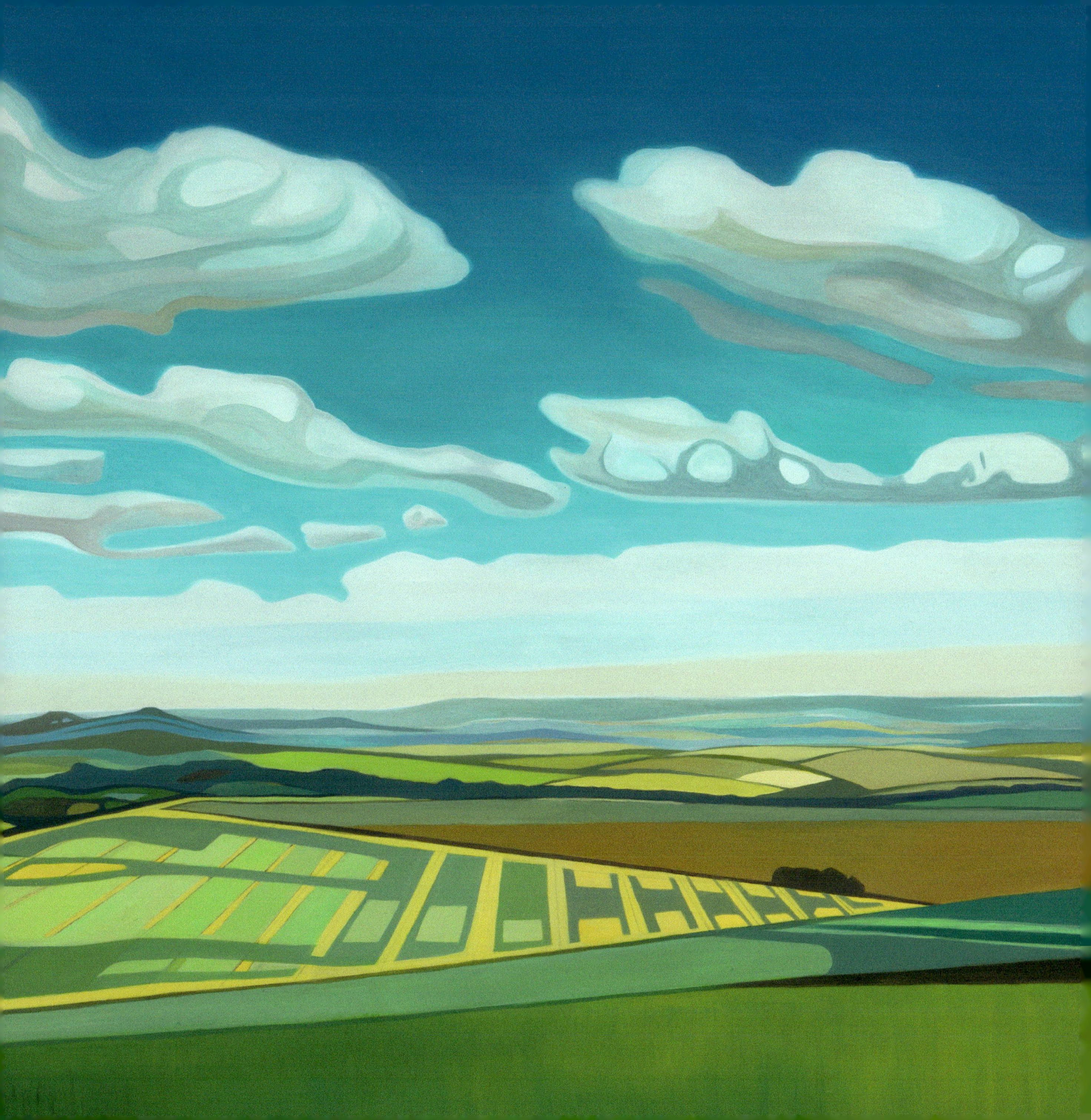

Towards Lowbury Hill

Near here two roads cross;
one plausibly the past, one
supposedly the future.

Where roads meet would be
a gibbet or a cairn or just
a stone; sometimes stalls

selling snacks. Continue on
or turn; a simple choice.
Parking up, I put on my boots,

lock the car, go east or west
and throw away the keys.

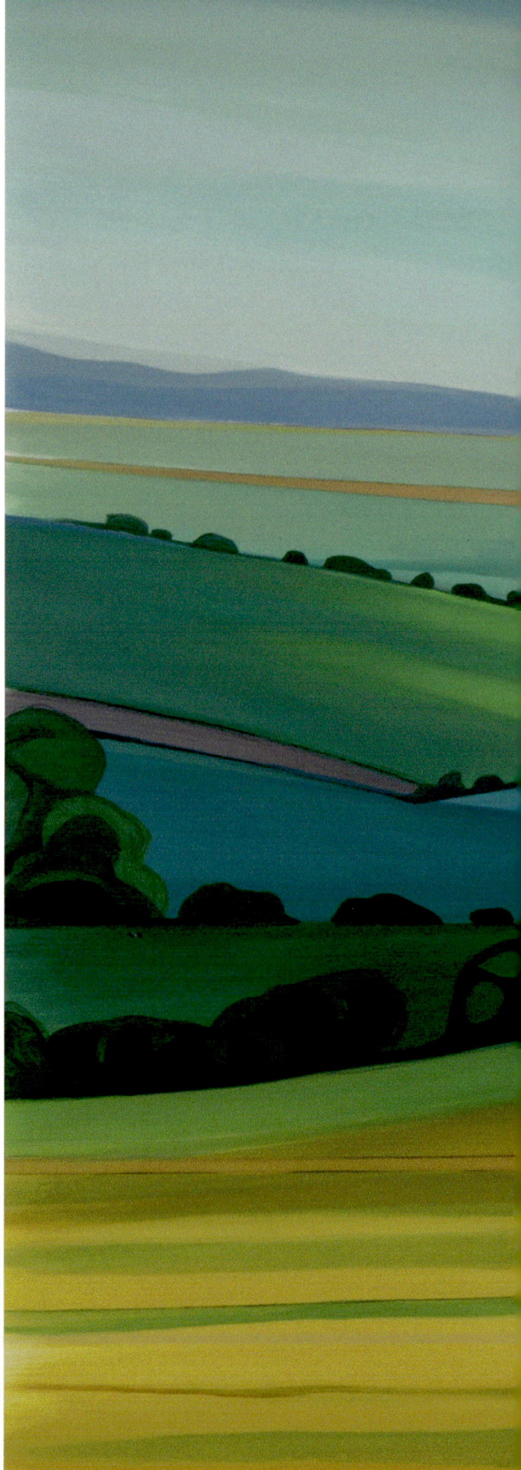

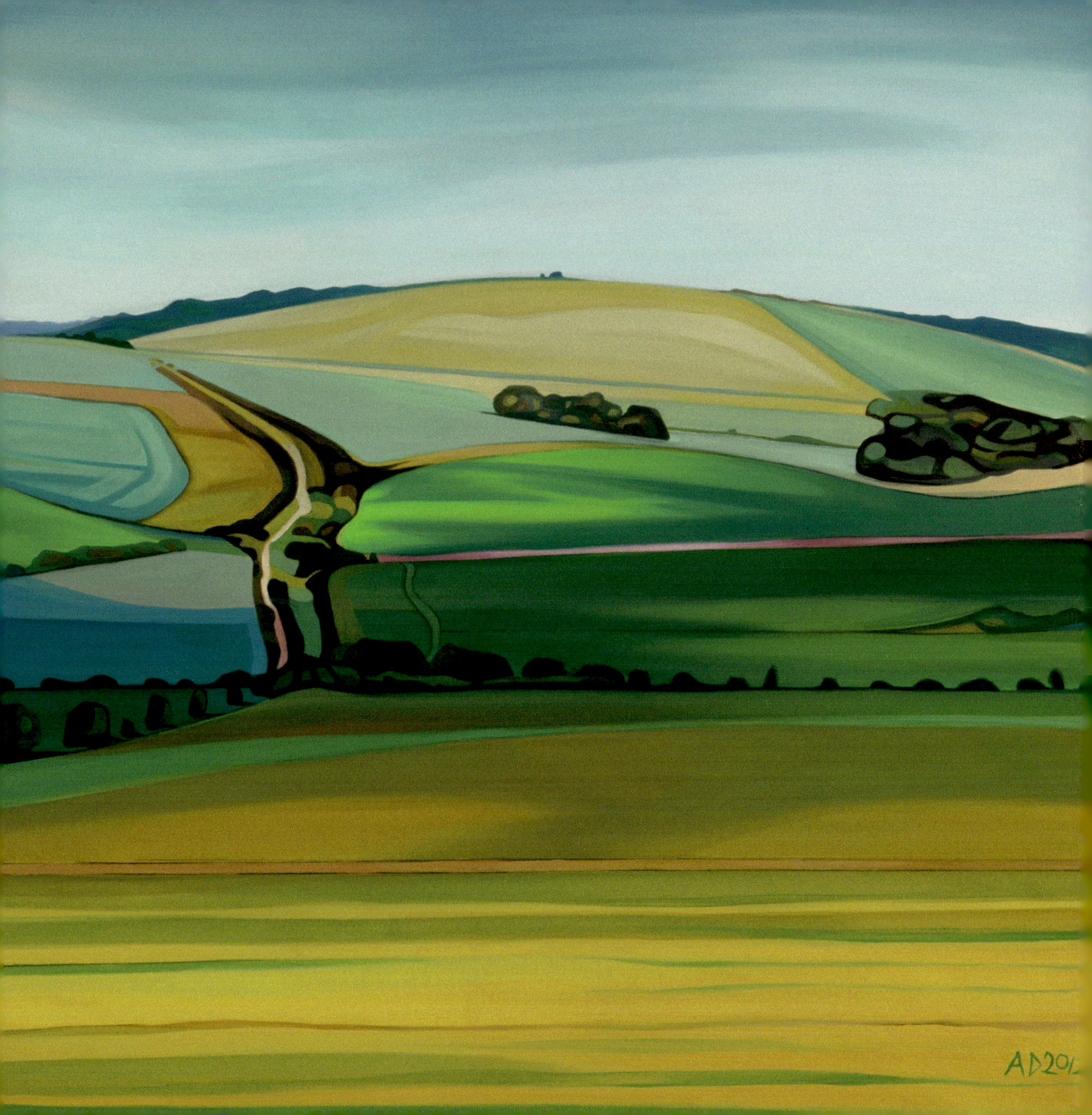

AD201

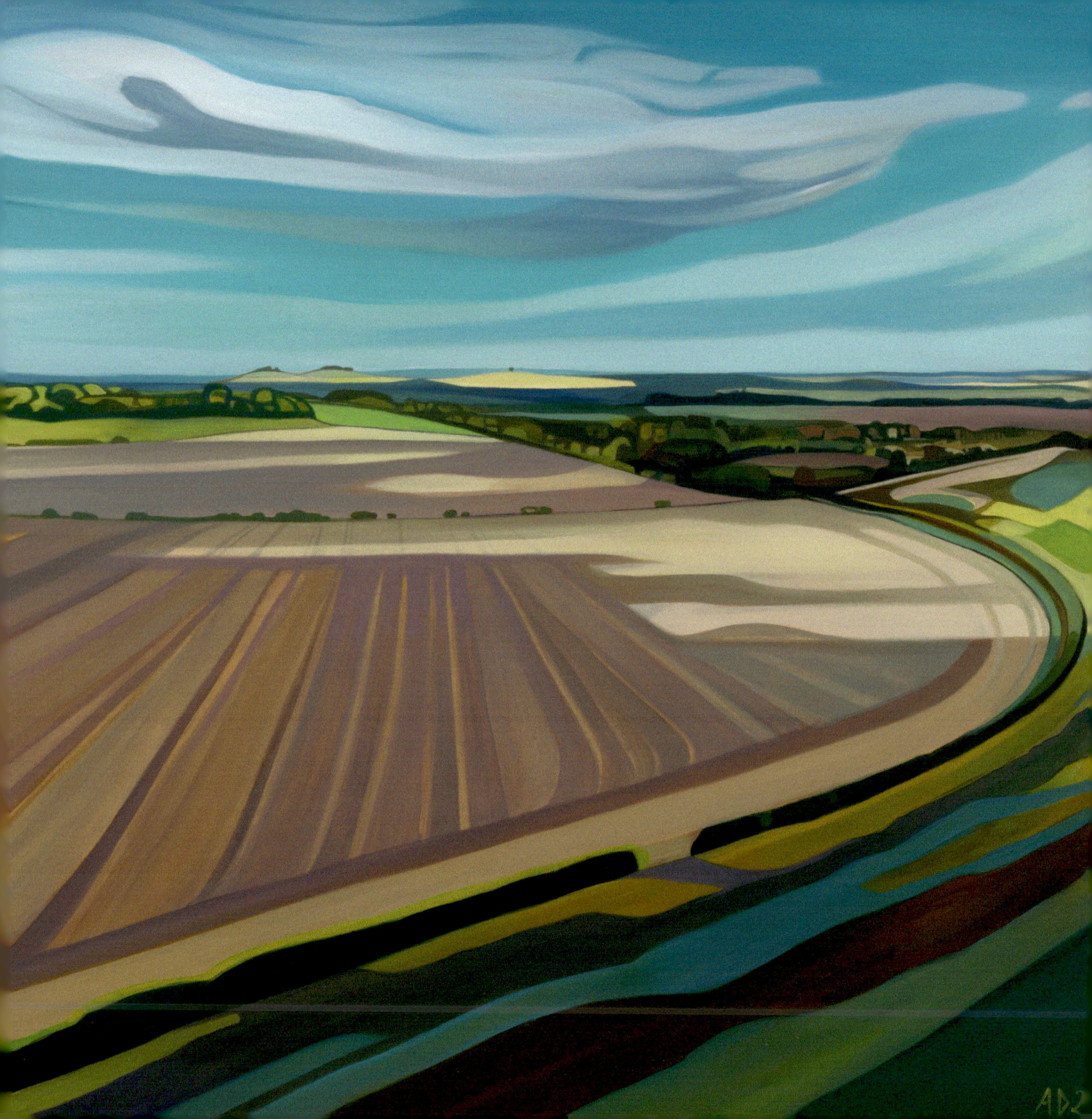

Lid Hill View

Landscape music. First a bass ground,
the masonry drill from a distance,
a dark deciduous green.

Then small melodies,
chainsaws or barbed wire rattling,
sharp swelling yellow, like fresh decay.

Then later, the brassy boom of an industrial process
involving silos or a metal door of a storage unit
being slammed shut repeatedly.

And at the mid-range, are cows lowing?
Yes, they are, for no apparent reason.
Low cows!

Lastly, a piece of flint dropped
into a deep chalk well, weeks
ago; and the waiting…

The Industrial Henge

i.m. Beryl Daphne Davidson

I approach from the south, finding a path
blanket-stitched against a hawthorn hedge.

A leaf is a tree, a field of winter wheat
is a strip of gold. No cows stare or plough

towards me as I cross the pale green pasture
towards the fat sad souls of cooling towers.

No coal trains make their merry-go-rounds.
No roads to follow into town, no town

to speak of. Everything that was, is not:
my mum and dad, my sister, the ginger cat.

Oh darling town, oh streets and people,
oh little apple tree in my back garden.

I held you in the hand of my content;
I hold you in the hand of my content.

The trains that supplied Didcot Power Station with Midlands coal
were called 'Merry-Go-Rounds'; the railway was laid in a large loop
and wagons loads were discharged without stopping.

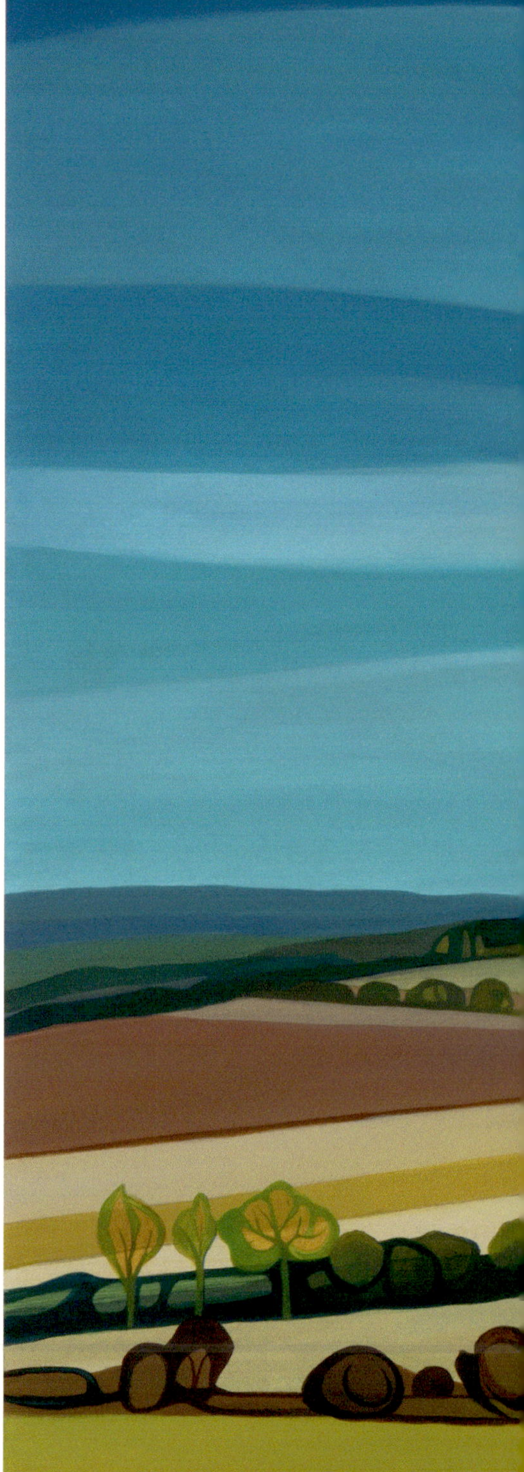

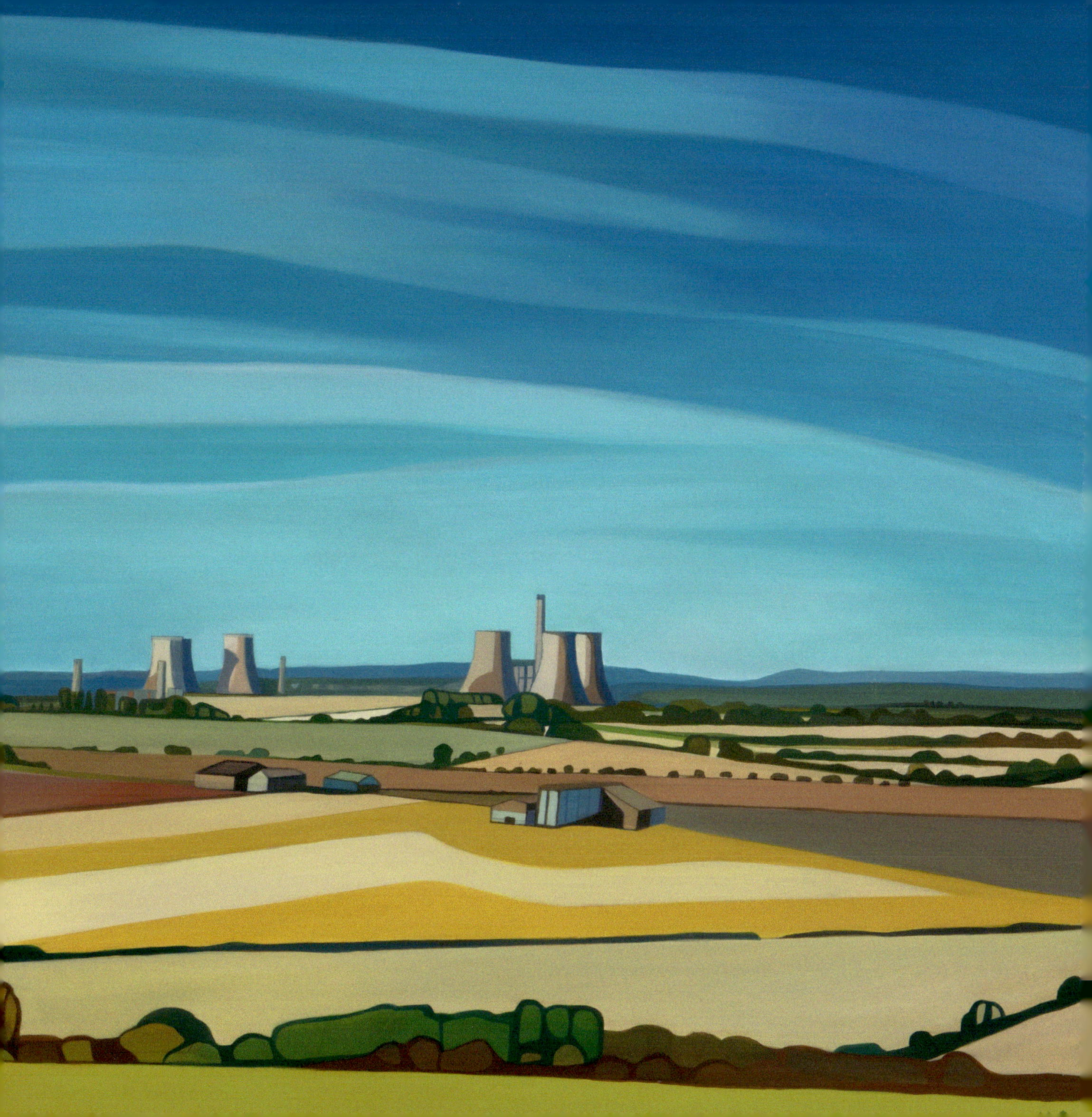

The Icknield Way

Nearly home now, our saddle bags sway
in strange unison, a father and son,
as we tap away the miles.

Dad will tell anyone who asks – and many
who don't – that he came this way in nineteen forty-nine
not knowing he'd later call it home.

A long ride from Liverpool, and he appears to be wearing
the same corduroy shorts, worn and corrugated
like fields of furry cabbages.

One day they stopped cycling together – the boy too old
to spend time with his old man, who looked daft
anyway, on a treader,

which was what we called bikes in Didcot in them days:
That you and your dad on your treaders, I saw Sunday,
Davidson?   *Nah, mate, not me.*

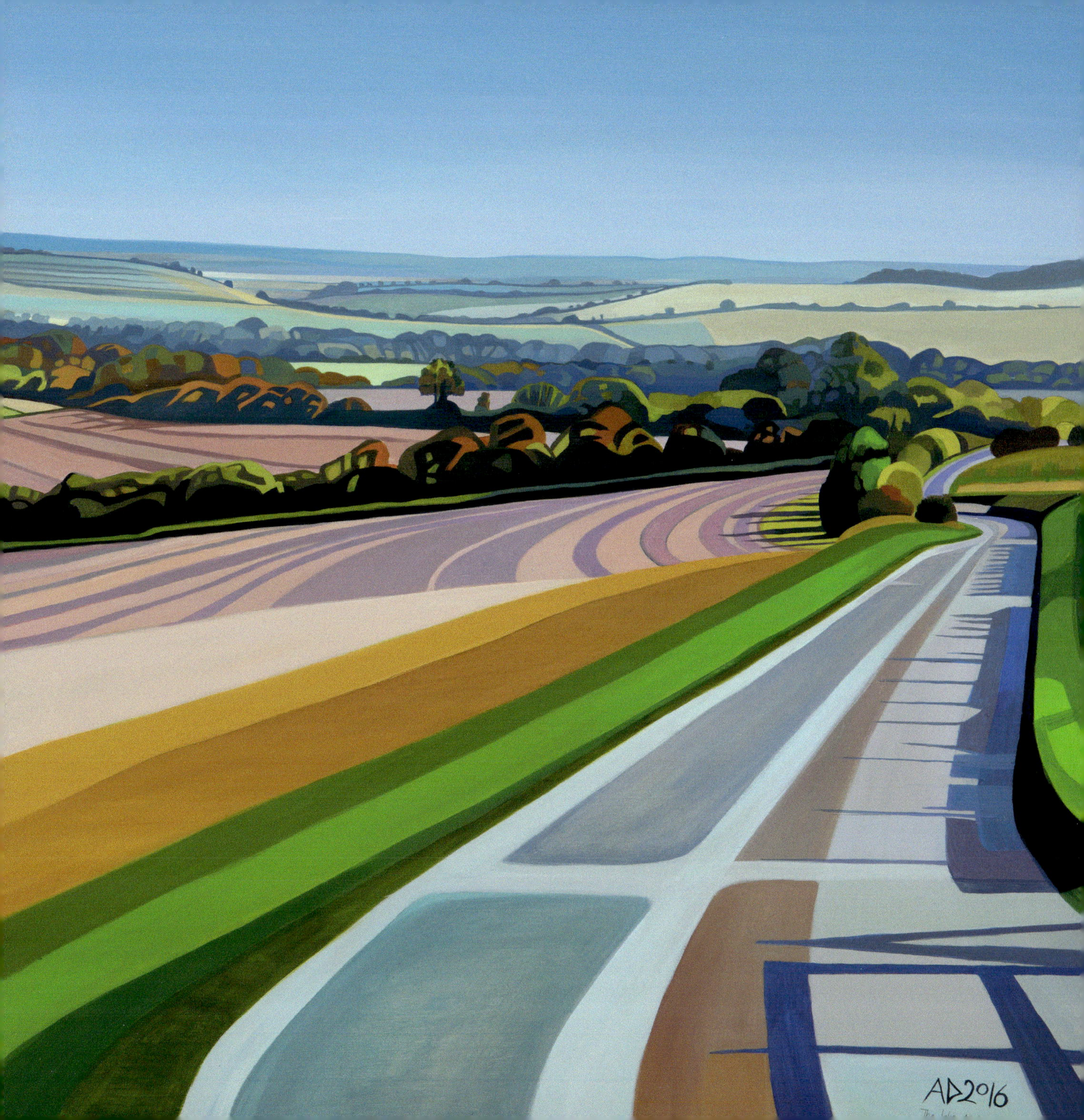

AD2016

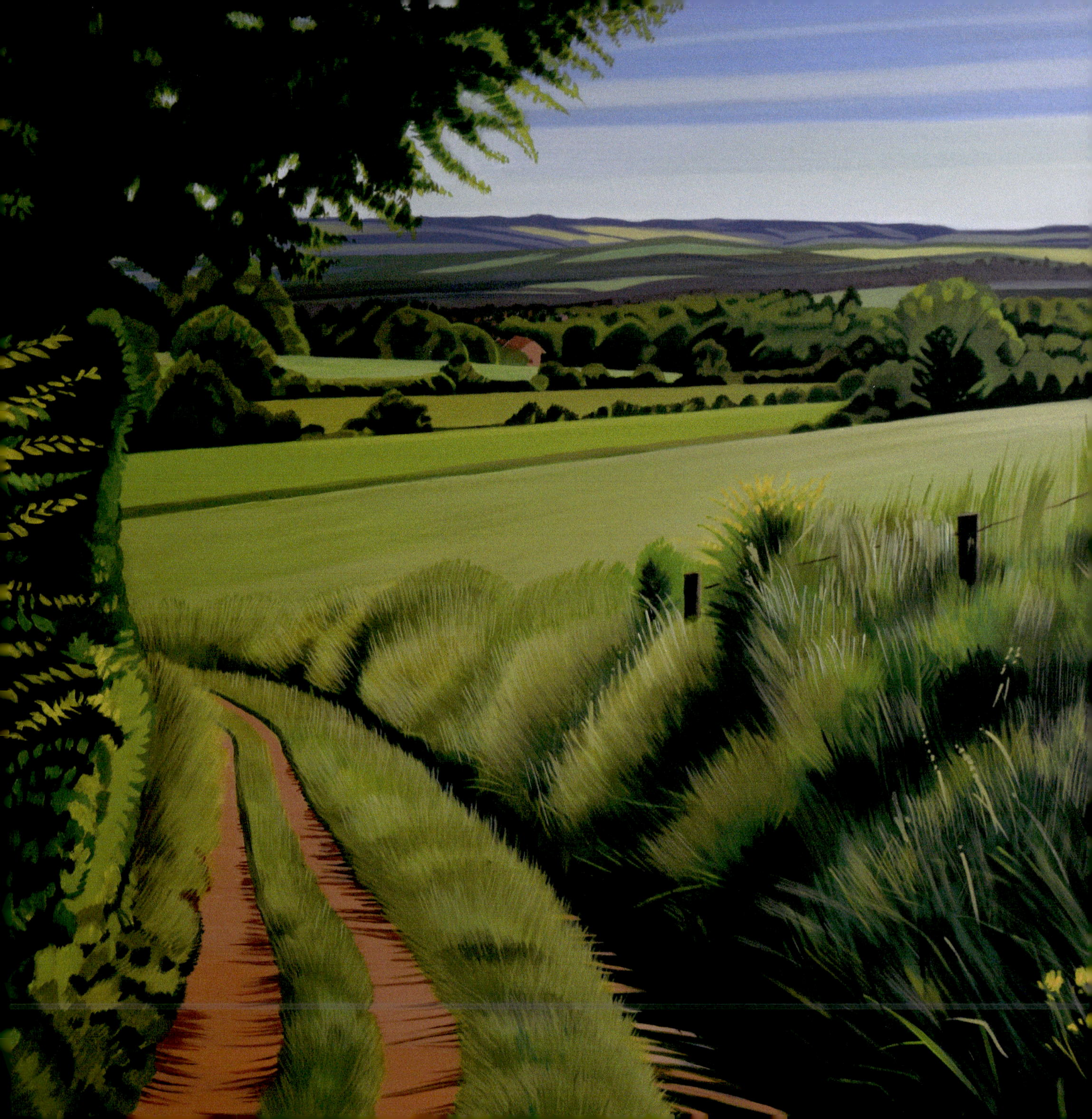

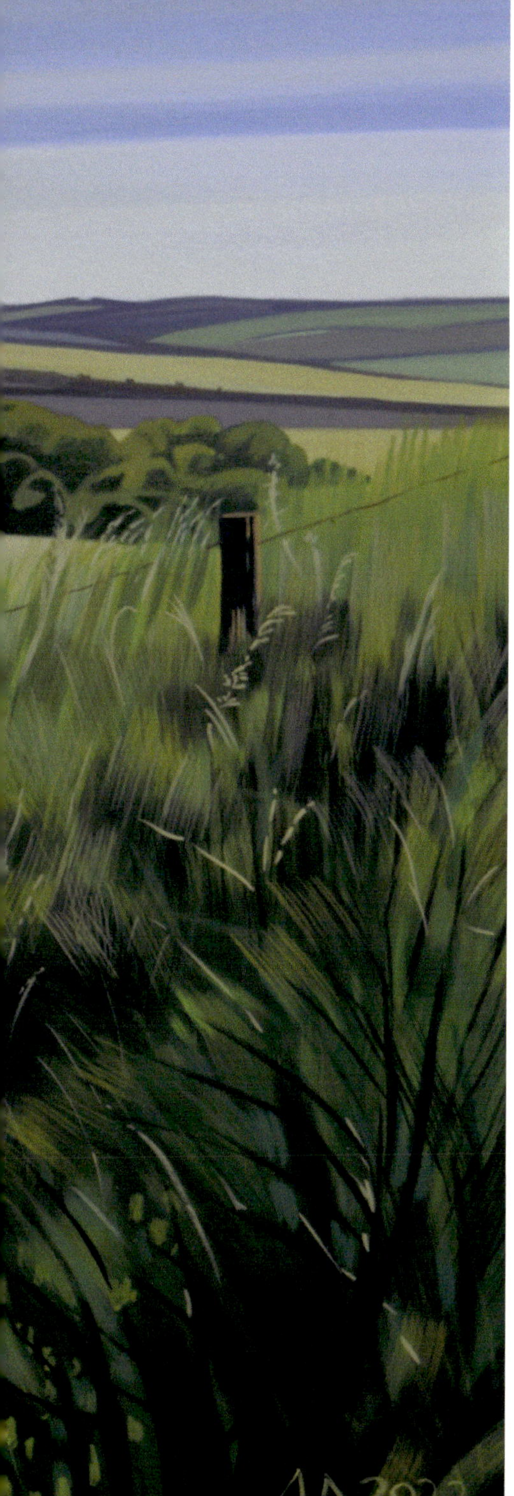

Three English Fields

i.m. David Hart, poet

When the world went, there was left only
the old tracks through fields. They call them
English, although they don't speak or fight
or do anything much. In memory of another
poet, I will find a body near here and
also I will drink tea from a flask and eat
my sandwiches. It is so quiet, still-ish.
It's not unpleasantly warm, although
it will be. When we're all gone, all come
to earth or air, this will be the last place
in England and then, uncultivated, these
will be the last English fields, their paths
and headlands all that remain of us.

The Anglo-Welsh poet David Hart spent most of his life in
the English Midlands. His poems sometimes include discovered
bodies, and often feature flasks of tea and sandwiches.

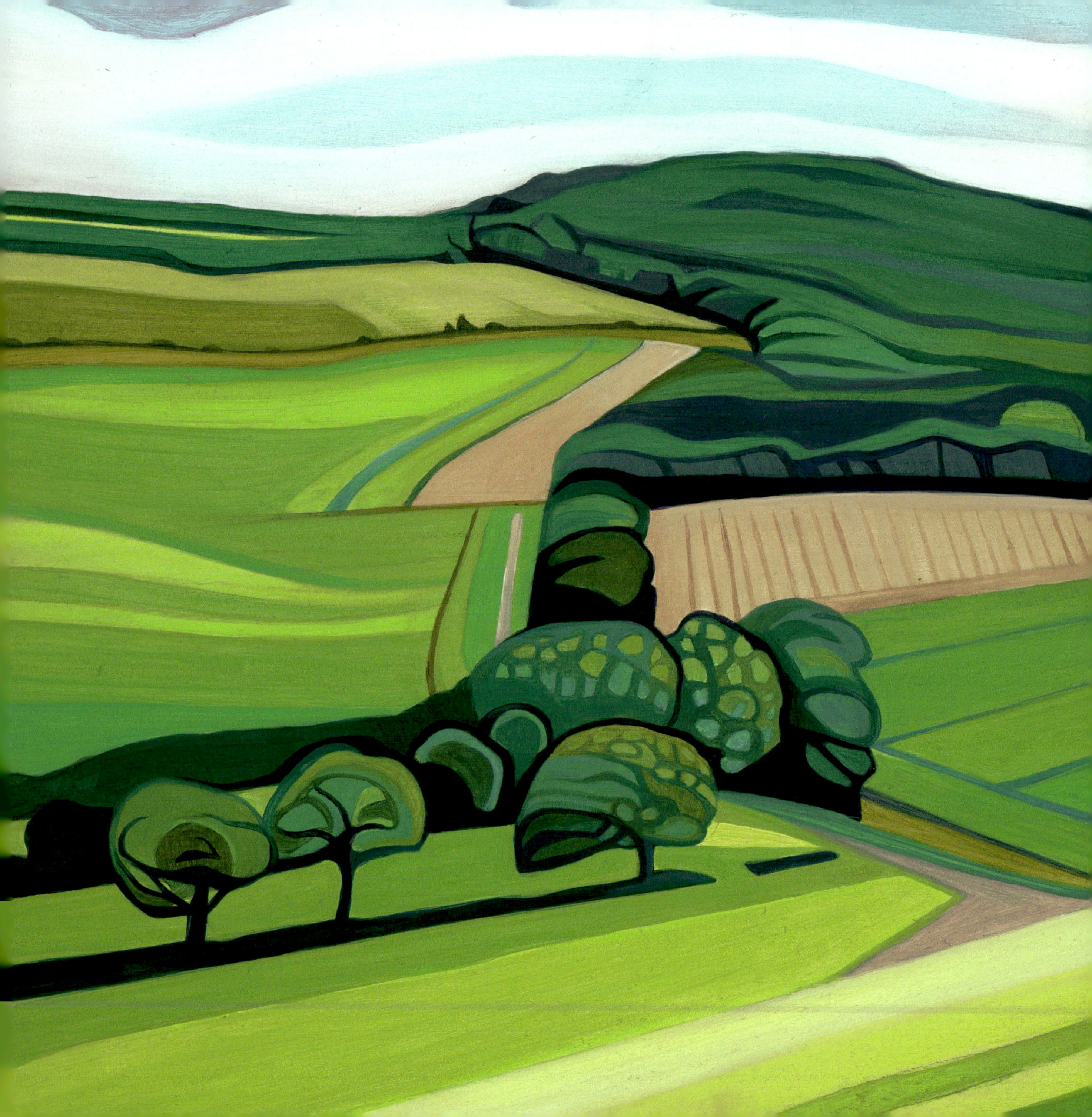

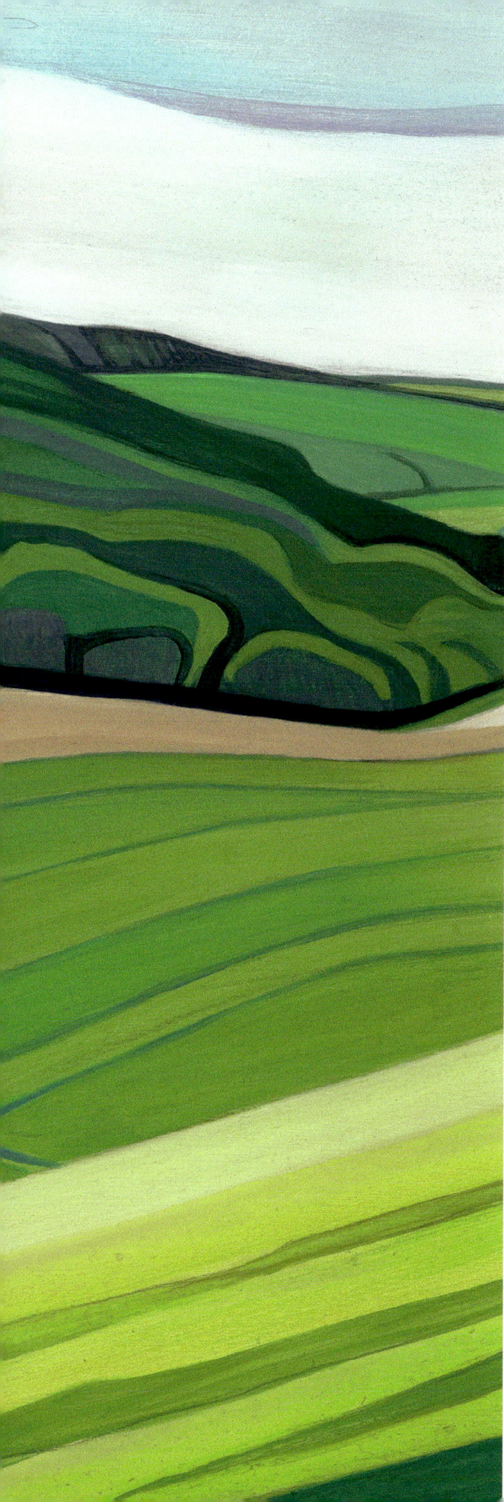

Unhill Woods

Went to hide in the Unhill Woods:
a green scab on a big boy's knee,
a kingdom for an exiled prince.

Took myself home, eventually,
having thought things through, having
sung myself into sullen silence.

Met no one, probably, kept my head
down; skulked or simply stood looking
up through the rain-shower of sunlight;

listened to the sea of green breaking
on the shore. One time didn't come back;
am still there now, lying among leaves.

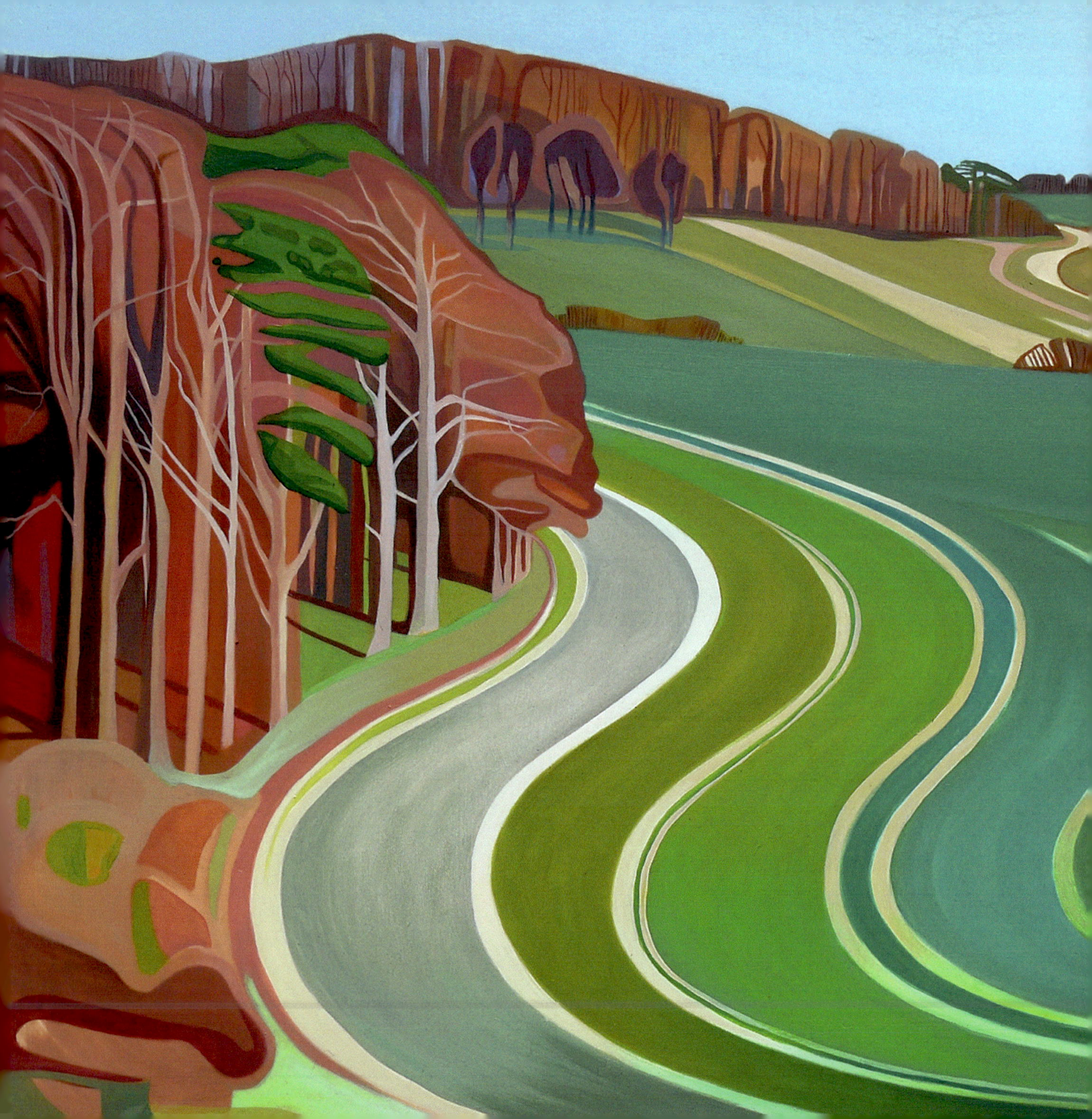

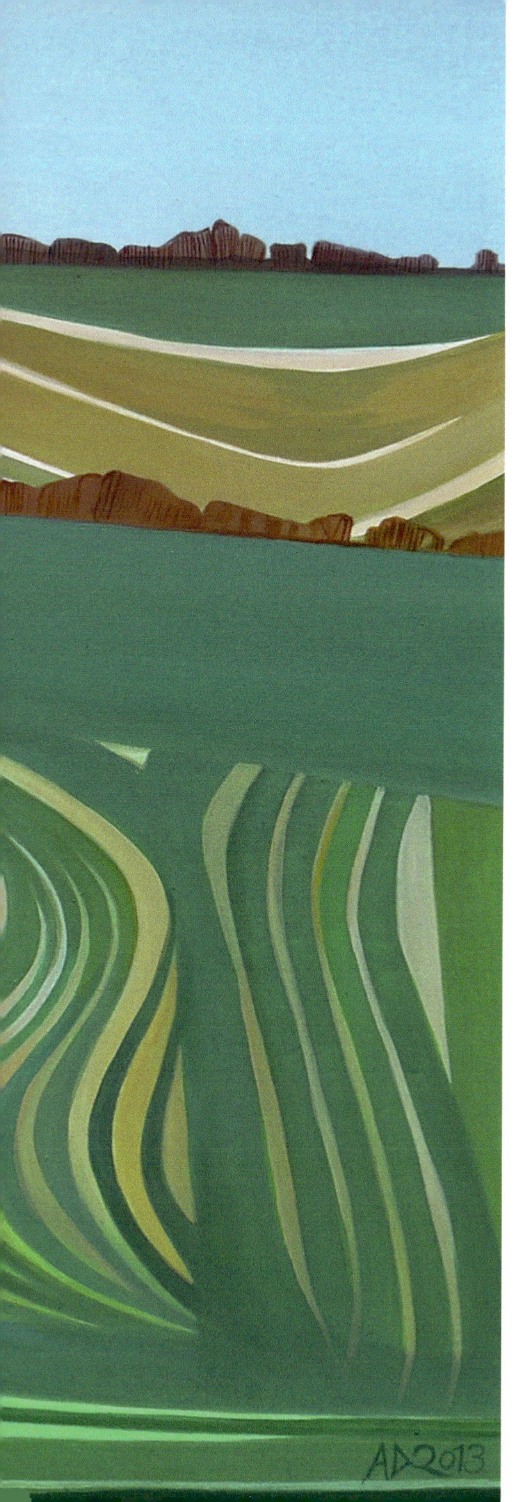

Juniper Hollow

Coming down from the Ashdown, through
the windblown woods, I find myself stood

adjacent to arable land, unrecognisable
but also familiar. It is nineteen eighty-two

and I am jobless, aimless, diligently reading
the *Making of the English Landscape* by W.

G. Hoskins for the fourth time, loving his
Saxon boundary ditches and Roman towns,

how he read the landscape like a book and
would have had something to say about this

anonymous spot, on the uses of juniper,
perhaps, or how past industriousness brought

wealth to one and destitution to another. Ah,
what people like my people once worked here,

what faith and labour filled their empty lives,
what weary joy they failed to write about.

The Making of the English Landscape (1954) by W.G. Hoskins
was a ground-breaking book, offering an approach to history
based on landscapes and the people who shaped them.

Kingstanding Hill

Coming towards me, coming
to meet me surely, through
what may be wheat, along
the poppy blood line.

Grey sunlight glints
on their spectacles
and wrist watches
or clouded canes, such
as carry them.

They are a grass rabble
with no order about them
at all, just their heads
nodding as they walk,
an army or congregation,
members of an association
associated with me.

And they come slowly
up the hill to greet me,
to make me welcome,
all my known people,

all my known people,
coming to meet me, walking
from the was, the used to be.

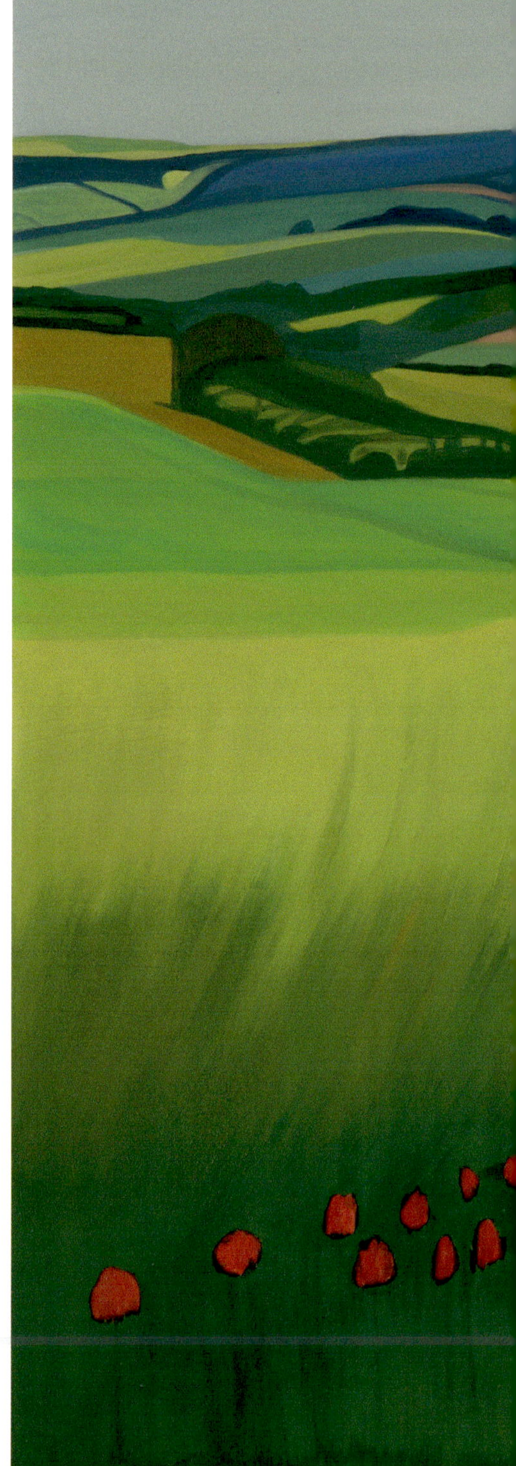

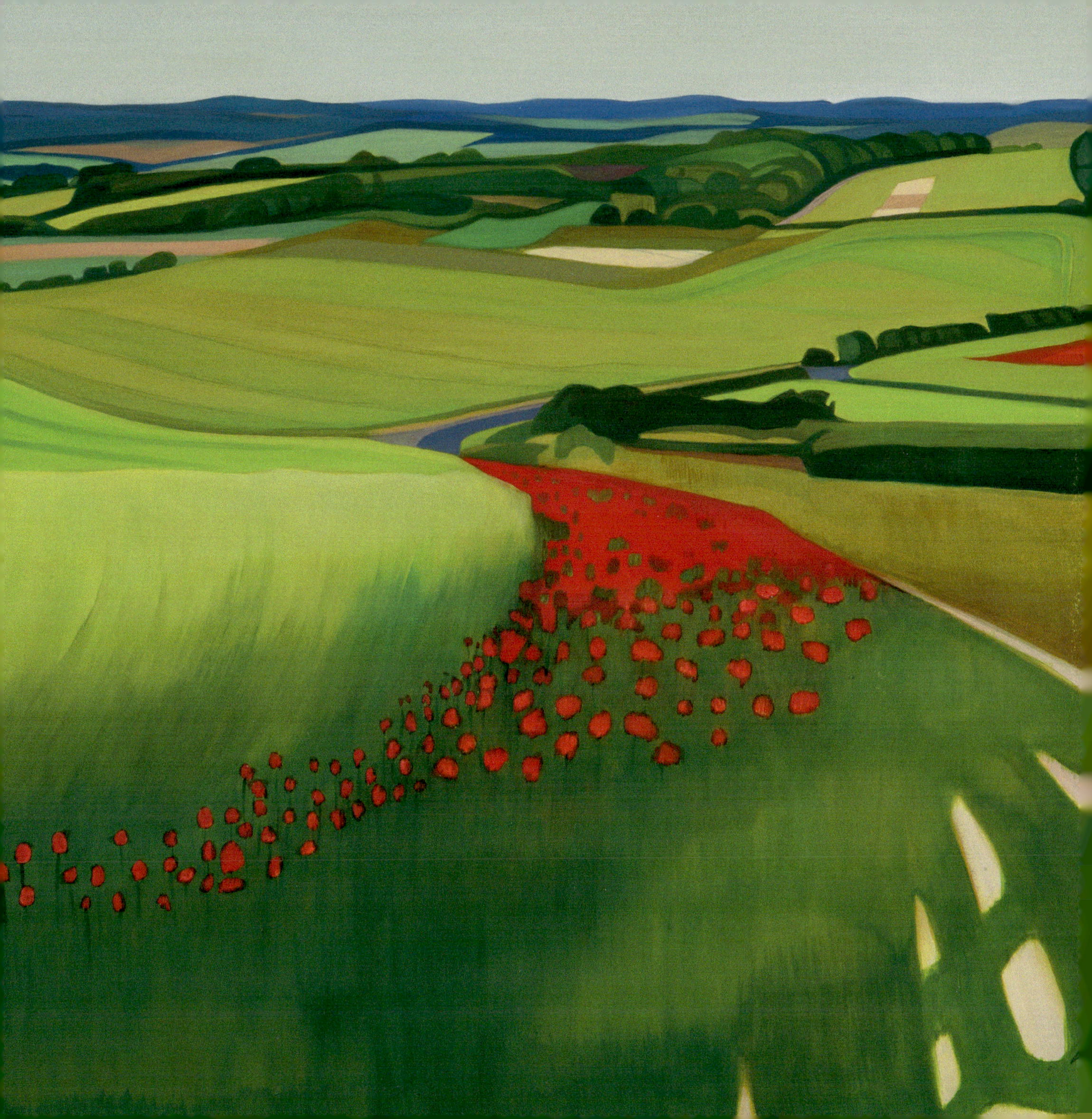

At the End – Two Cyclists

When the last wheel
has buckled and the last
derailleur has seized itself solid,
we'll burn our maps and shake clean
our memories of summer to summer.

We'll carry ourselves out –
while there's hardly light in the sky –
and hide where we can, in the field of wheat
or else in the beautiful, autumnal,
metallic clump of beech trees on the hill.

Finis

Talking about *Downland*

In October 2023, Jonathan spoke to Anna about her relationship with the Downs, and in the course of the conversation shared some of his own thoughts on what makes this landscape so productive for writers and artists.

Setting the scene…

Jonathan [JD]   For me *Downland* is a book of beautiful paintings with some words (Anna, you may see it slightly differently!), but certainly the focus is our connections with what we still call the Berkshire Downs. I know that as we speak you are sitting near to your studio, a mile or so away from the Downs. So, you're very close to the subject matter, aren't you?

Anna [AD]   The Ridgeway from where I'm sat right now is about 40 minutes' walk away, all uphill. I'm in the village of Aston Tirrold.

Personal histories…

JD   This stretch we're talking about is the Middle Ridgeway between Streatley – where the River Thames cuts through a line of hills – going west towards just above Swindon. When I was growing up in Didcot, this was the part of the Downs I would go to. I went first with my dad, who was a keen cyclist – he wanted his children to be keen cyclists, particularly his son.

So, from the age of six or seven, I was on bike rides with my dad, trailing behind him. I distinctly remember, at the age of eight, the first time I was able to climb up onto the Downs without getting off my bike. We would cycle out on a Sunday across the clay vale south of Didcot, and then up onto the Downs, through East Ilsley, West Ilsley, Aldworth, all those villages.

So, the Downs have always been in my mind, and if you live in Didcot – and I know you went to school in Didcot, Anna – depending on the light, the Downs either appear very low on the horizon or as these towering mountains. So that's my story about the Downs.

Well, what about you? When did the Downs start to come into your work?

AD   Well, I like to think that the connection I have with the Downs and the Ridgeway is something that I've always had because I went to school in Avebury and then I moved here, at about the age of seven, to Aston Tirrold – although I was born in Wallingford, on the Thames. So, the Ridgeway connects the places where I've lived.

When you were talking about Didcot and cycling with your father, I was thinking of going on a school bus to Didcot and travelling through all the villages. I was always staring out of the window. I was the sort of kid that would sit on their own daydreaming. And as you meandered around the villages you are always catching glimpses of chalk downland.

Also, my grandparents, who lived in the village, were avid walkers, so we were dragged out for long walks on Sundays. I liked the fact that we would walk up the Downs. As a child I never quite understood why they were called the Downs – I was definitely walking up them. Connected to the village are the Aston Downs, and further on, the Blewbury Downs, and these connect to the Churn Estate, so we have the feeling of lovely open landscape.

The Downs in detail…

JD   I know your father is something of a scholar of the Middle Ridgeway, with a knowledge of so many facets of this area of countryside. How did his interest in the Downs affect you?

AD   He walked the Ridgeway with his brother-in-law in the 1970s, including the stretch we're talking about. They did it as two young lads with backpacks, unsuitable footwear, no water, and I don't think they finished it all, between you and me, but they had a lot of fun en route. I remember him talking about this epic walk, and I was always very interested in doing that myself.

He also had a knowledge of chalk downlands because he was an ecologist. So, on walks he encouraged my sister and I to look at the nature around us, at the biodiversity. So, I've always had that kind of visual connection to the landscape through him. Very much so.

JD   You and I know this landscape very well and I have the reality of it in my mind. But I also have a version of it from your paintings and you may have some versions of it through my words. But for people who don't know what the Middle Ridgeway is like, I wonder how we would describe this landscape. Anna, as you're the visual artist, could you describe this landscape?

AD   It's very much a farmed landscape now, very arable, very open, and it provides us with incredible panoramic views across the Thames Valley and the Vale of the White Horse. There's an incredible network of footpaths and old drovers' roads—even I get lost at certain points up there, when there's five or six tracks intertwining across the Ridgeway.

You get a feeling of escapism. You get a feeling of being solitary in the landscape. It's very relaxing, but it's also inspirational. You're constantly looking. The light up there is really quite something. In all weathers, even like today, which is a bit murky because we've had a storm, it is dramatic.

JD   Yes, you're right. I've spent the last two years reminding myself that this part of the world isn't what people imagine the South of England to be. It's not shopping centres and gastropubs. It is actually rather wild. Hardly anybody lives on the Downs because of the lack of water. Villages are mostly located at the foot of the Downs or further down the dip slope towards the River Kennet.

It really is a lonely place, which makes the sheer quantity of tracks and footpaths slightly ghostly. That there must have been so much traffic up there at one point, presumably 2,000 years ago. I've often been up on the Downs and there's been literally no one else in sight, which given you're only two miles from Didcot Parkway Railway Station is impressive.

Artists of the Downs…

JD   That emptiness you've mentioned makes me want to ask you about your artistic influences. How have you developed as an artist, and how have you come to produce these very vivid, hyper-realistic paintings?

AD   My influences and inspiration come from 20th century British artists, like Paul Nash. I also love his brother's work—John Nash—who was the lesser known of the two at the time but has now gained better recognition. There's also, obviously, Eric Ravilious who painted, so brilliantly, the chalk downland landscape and managed to capture the quality of that light we we're talking about.

I have a book, edited by Richard Ingrams to accompany a Ridgeway exhibition in Swindon in the 1980s, of an amazing series of artists. I flicked through this book as a child, and I was absolutely in awe of all the work. There is one painting, by a chap called Patrick Malacarnet from Jersey. It's a beautiful panorama of the Uffington White Horse. This book and the exhibition had a profound effect on me.

JD   That painting could be an 'early Anna Dillon'. There is an almost a geometric analysis of the landscape. There is order but a disorder also.

Subverting the genre…

JD   As an aside, one of the things that drew me to your paintings was the fact that human life is hidden. We see the fields, we see Didcot Power Station – now gone – and the odd building, but generally your landscapes are depopulated, as if they are prelapsarian – before the fall or after the apocalypse. This gives me space to write, so thank you; but why do your paintings focus on the non-human?

AD   Probably, if I'm being frank, the Victorian genre of landscape painting always included people who were working the landscape but I feel like those paintings have become a little bit 'chocolate boxey'. I didn't feel that adding the human element into the landscape added anything. For me, it's the love of the landscape, how it has been shaped by humans rather than the humans themselves.

JD   Yes. The centre of gravity is the land and the colours and shapes. I've always been struck by – and I've responded to it in one of the poems – the extraordinary range of colours you use for what I would say is just like green or grey. I know you're not doing a photographic reproduction of what you see – you're doing a version of it filtered through your imagination – but would you say a little bit about your use of colour?

AD   There's an Austrian artist people might be familiar with, Friedensreich Hundertwasser, who produces beautifully coloured work. His bold, primary colours inspired me.

But here I'm going to pay credit to my former art teacher of Didcot Girls' School, Ron Freeborn, who sadly passed away a few years ago. He was a phenomenal art teacher and has left an amazing legacy of artists inspired and encouraged by him. He taught us to paint and not be afraid of colour. He taught us colour by looking at the Impressionists' work. He taught us to look beyond what was there to see colours that other people might miss.

JD   That's interesting, because when I've responded to your paintings with poems, I've resisted the urge to simply describe the painting. I've been thrown into trying to describe what is beyond the painting, a personal response. My late father is with me, of course, because he dragged me up to the Downs and he is present in my life.

More about fathers...

AD   Did your father have an influence on you becoming a poet, apart from being able to connect to the landscape?

JD   He was evacuated when he was 12 to North Wales and lived in a Welsh speaking community and didn't really speak Welsh. So that made him a lonely and slightly troubled boy. And he was probably a lonely and slightly troubled man throughout his life. But he loved to perform and was a great dancer and he loved to sing as we were cycling, which was excruciating if you're 11 and your father is singing as you cycle. So, I inherited from him a desire to be heard and to entertain people and to create.

A writer's response...

JD   But let me ask you another question, Anna. I know you wouldn't call yourself a literary person, but your studio is full of books, often about the physical world you've painted. How has it been to have someone else write in response to your paintings?

AD   I am happy to confess that I'm quite dyslexic, which I think is reasonably common when you use the creative part of your mind. I wish I could be a good writer, but I'm not. I greatly admire people who have this skill and I'm drawn to your poetry because the landscape is being seen from two perspectives, with the link being our personal love of this landscape.

JD   Thank you very much. It has been an absolute pleasure, of course, but also it has caused me to get to know the painters who inspired you to understand where you've come from. And perhaps we have had a similar journey through the English tradition in the way we have responded to a non-urban landscape.

It has also been fascinating to see something of how you make a painting, the sheer physical hard work it takes. And you have made so many wonderful paintings, mostly, not exclusively, of the chalk hills of the south of England and in that tradition of landscape painting.

So, let me ask, where are you going now? How are you developing your art?

Future directions…

AD   I'm embedded in the landscape. There is nothing I'd sooner do than continue to paint landscapes. I've become a big walker. Walking and painting mesh together. There's so much of the British Isles that I want to see, walking and then painting. I've recently collaborated with a drone pilot, Hedley Thorne. We've just finished the Wessex Airscapes Wiltshire exhibition at the Wiltshire Museum.

I've also abstracted a bit with some of my work, collaging and mono-printing, which has enabled me to have a smaller, looser style of work, which is stepping away from the control required by the large oil paintings. So that's really fun and it's quite exciting as a new medium. I'm loving it because it's risky, you don't know where it's going, it's hit and miss. It is really dynamic. And what, what about you, Jonathan?

JD   Well, I never know after one book what I'm doing next. And you never know if there's going to be another book because the poetry world is full of ups and downs. I'm probably, possibly heading in the other direction for you, in that I'm more and more interested in form and the restrictions that form places upon you and the outcomes as a result. This means you write much more slowly because you write in a highly formulaic way, working away at the same block of text, draft after draft.

But like walking along the Berkshire Downs on the Ridgeway, there are many little paths to take if one wishes, but the old road goes on and we simply follow it.

Further reading and useful links

More about Anna, Jonathan & Two Rivers Press

http://www.annadillon.com
https://jonathandavidson.net
https://tworiverspress.com

The Ridgeway National Trail

https://www.nationaltrail.co.uk/en_GB/trails/the-ridgeway
https://www.northwessexdowns.org.uk/visitor-information/
https://ridgewayfriends.org.uk

History, Geology, Flora & Fauna

https://www.nationaltrail.co.uk/en_GB/trails/the-ridgeway/historic_ridgeway
https://www.northwessexdowns.org.uk/the-landscape/geology
https://www.northwessexdowns.org.uk/the-landscape/biodiversity

Writers & Artists

https://www.nationaltrail.co.uk/en_GB/top_50_writers
https://www.nationaltrail.co.uk/en_GB/top_50_artists
https://www.littletoller.co.uk/authors/w-g-hoskins
https://hundertwasser.com/en

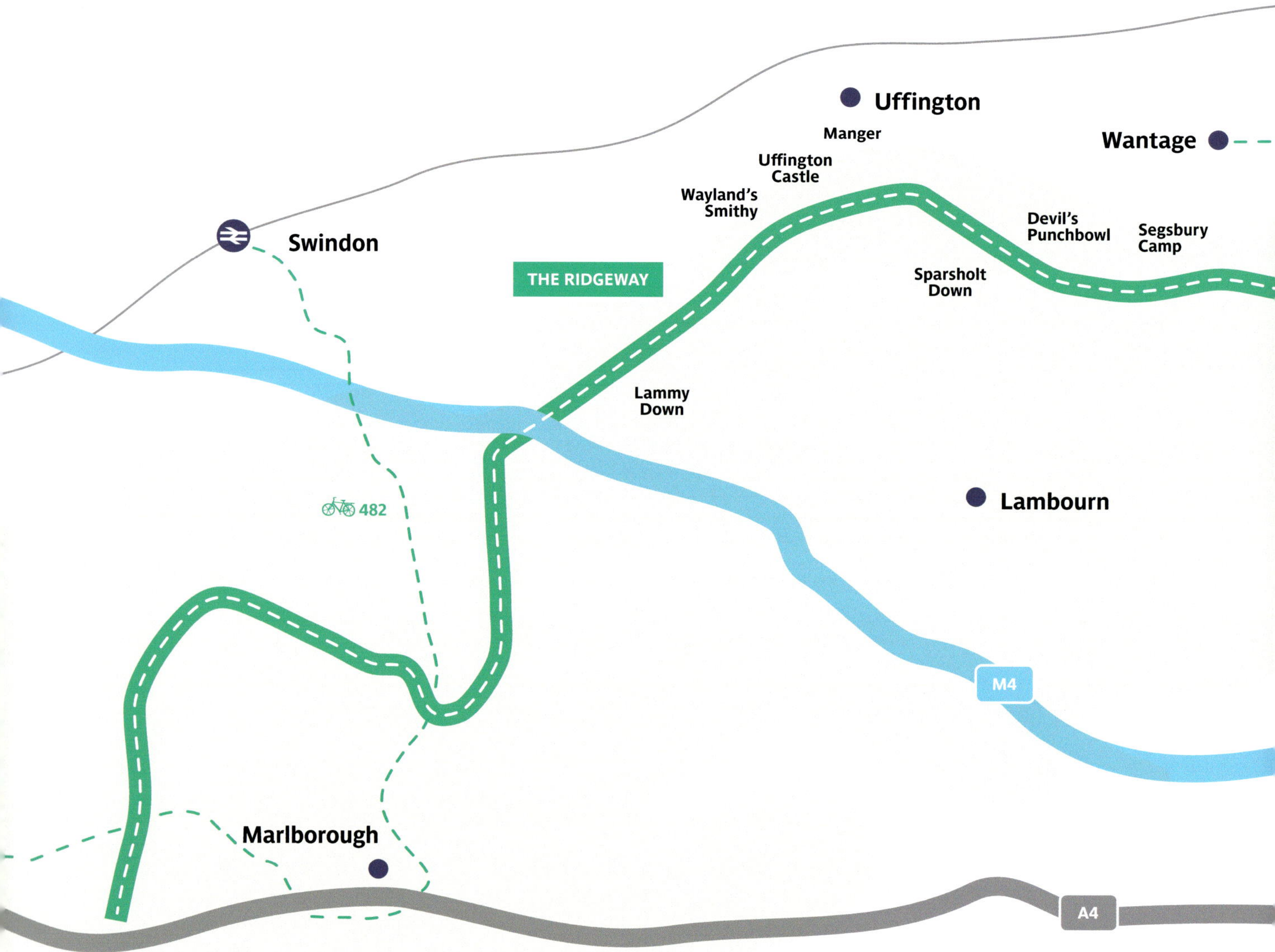
Uffington
Manger
Wantage
Uffington Castle
Wayland's Smithy
Devil's Punchbowl
Segsbury Camp
Swindon
THE RIDGEWAY
Sparsholt Down
Lammy Down
482
Lambourn
M4
Marlborough
A4

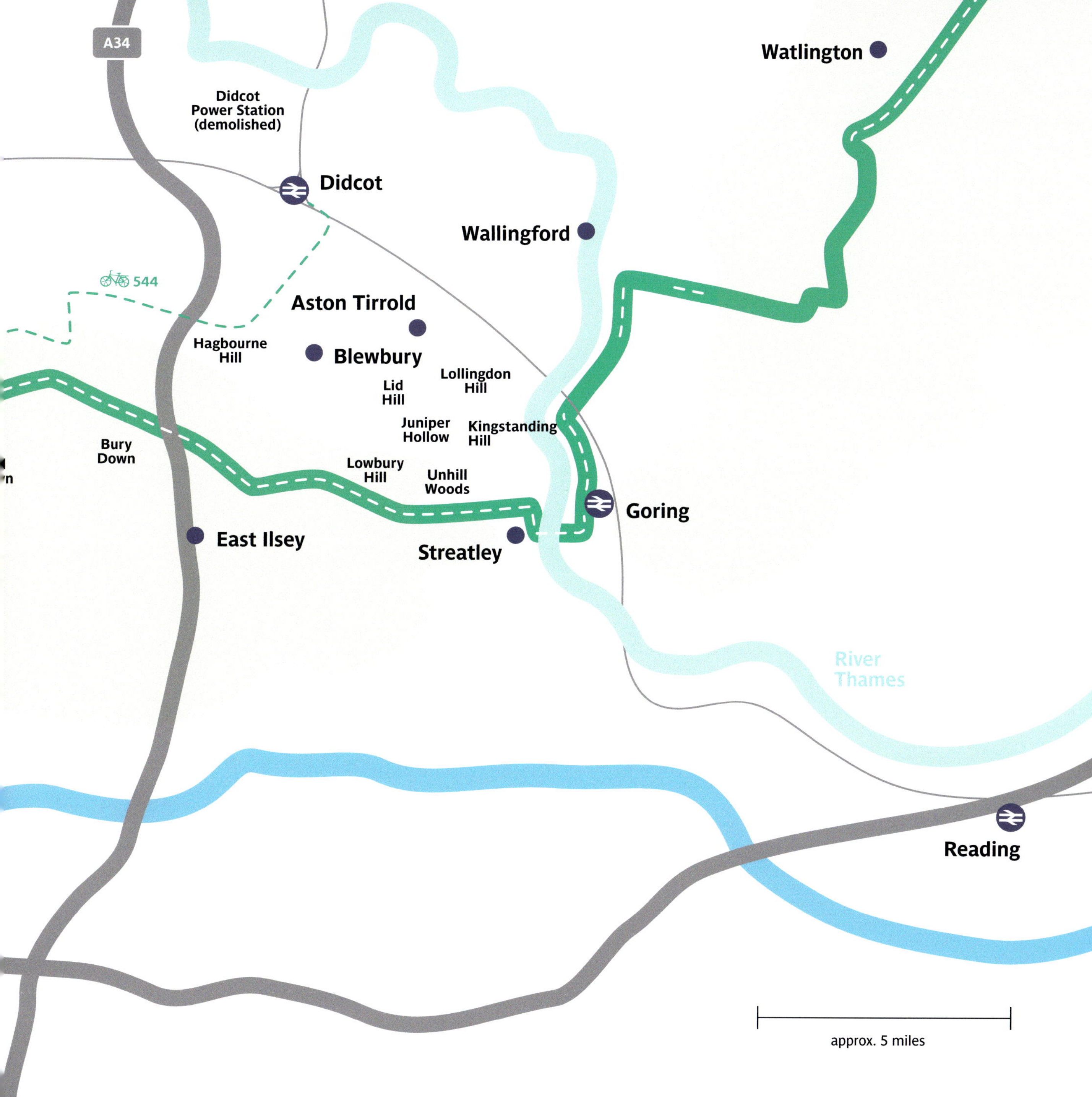

A34
Didcot Power Station (demolished)
Didcot
Watlington
Wallingford
544
Aston Tirrold
Hagbourne Hill
Blewbury
Lollingdon Hill
Lid Hill
Juniper Hollow
Kingstanding Hill
Bury Down
Lowbury Hill
Unhill Woods
East Ilsey
Streatley
Goring
River Thames
Reading
approx. 5 miles

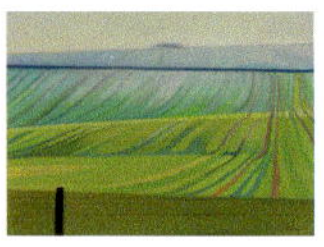

Lammy Down (2012)
Oil on board, 580 mm × 700 mm

This view is seen from The Ridgeway National Trail looking due South towards Lammy Down.

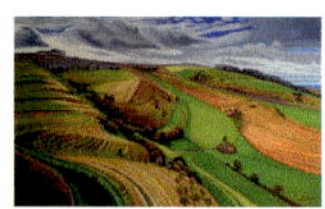

Rams Hill Coombe (2021)
Oil on board, 660 mm × 1000 mm

/// truffles.boomer.drip

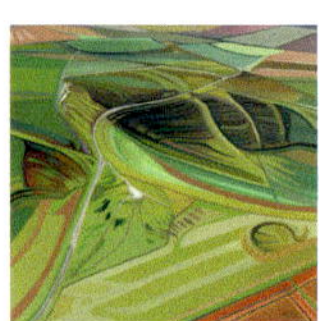

The Aerial Horse (2014)
Oil on board, 960 mm × 980 mm

An aerial view of White Horse Hill

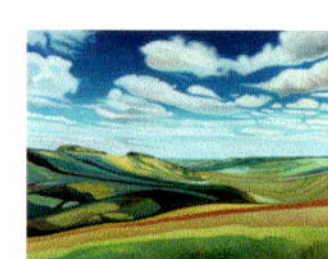

The Devil's Delight (2011)
Oil on board, 970 mm × 1170 mm
Mr Patrick Malaperiman [Private collection]

The Devil's Punchbowl in May

SU 34843 84895
/// hydrant.kickbacks.sour

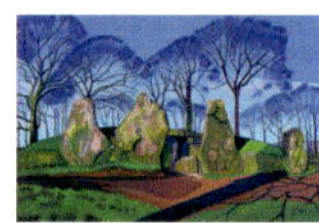

Wayland's Smithy (2016)
Oil on board, 750 mm × 880 mm

Painted from reference photos taken on a crisp, cold winter's day

SU 28092 8541
/// install.relished.lectured

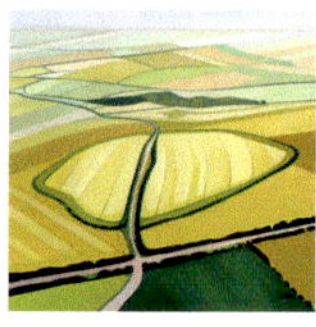

Segsbury Camp (2014)
Oil on board, 600 mm × 600 mm

An aerial view of the Iron Age Hill fort of Segsbury Camp near Wantage

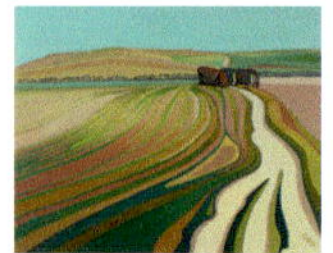

Towards Uffington (2012)
Oil on board, 795 mm × 905 mm
Richard & Rebecca Couzens [Private collection]

The famous view of Uffington Castle as seen from the Ridgeway

SU 28782 85670
/// shorts.grunt.resettle

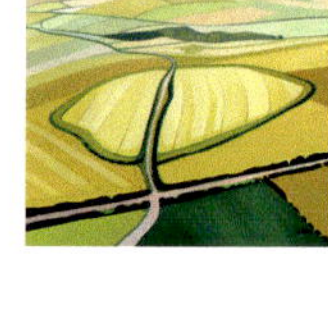

Farnborough View (2016)
Oil on board, 455 mm × 608 mm
Henrietta and Cormac Smyth [Private collection]

A commission of the Berkshire Down

SU 44335 82799
/// bashed.flocking.gravitate

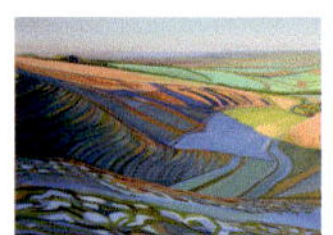

Frost on the Manger (2015)
Oil on board, 180 mm × 300 mm
Robert Mullan [Private collection]

A private commission of the Manger at Uffington White Horse

SU 30086 86726
/// remotes.nation.poses

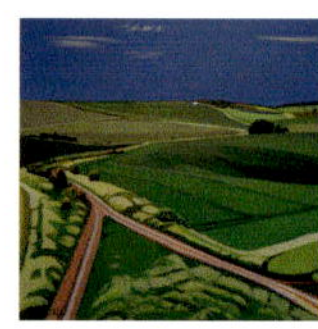

Old Down (2021)
Oil on board, 510 mm × 510 mm

/// done.norms.dispensed

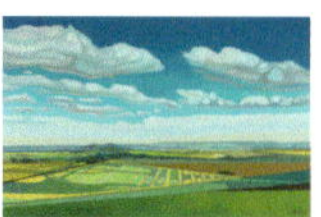

Bury Down (Ridgeway Series, 2012)
Oil on board, 870 mm × 1150 mm
Gillian Miners [Private collection]

Ridgeway view from near East Illsey

 SU 48415 83795
 taster.gurgling.crossing

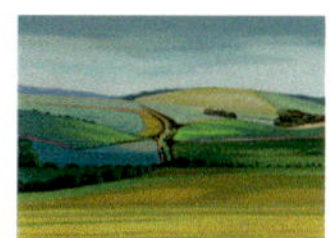

Towards Lowbury Hill (Ridgeway Series, 2012)
Oil on board, 790 mm × 880 mm
Barbara Allen [Private collection]

Ridgeway view from Compton Downs

 SU 51292 82079
 vesting.steroids.hedge

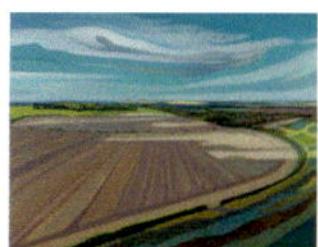

Lid Hill View (2013)
Oil on board, 710 mm × 790 mm

This view can be seen via Open Access dowland above Aston Tirrold

 SU 54893 85009
 shame.royally.confused

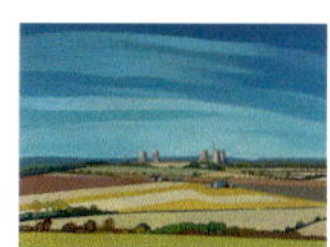

The Industrial Henge (2012)
Oil on board, 790 mm × 990 mm
Ricardo Fernandez [Private collection]

View of Didcot Power Station from Hagbourne Hill, before its demolition

 SU 49968 86970
 sparks.crank.ledge

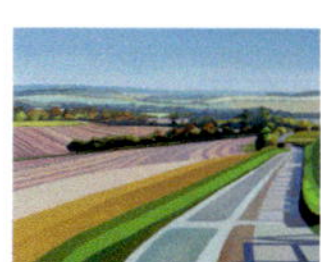

The Icknield Way (2016)
Oil on board, 605 mm × 720 mm

View of the Icknied Way above Upton Village

 SU 49784 87052
 blitz.stolen.buffoon

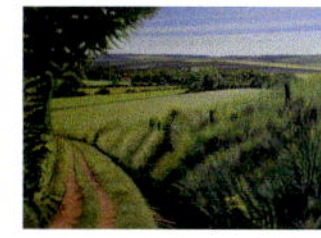

Three English Fields (2022)
Oil on board, 760 mm × 850 mm

A chalk track heading down from Lollingdon Hill
Nicky Whitaker [Private collection]

 SU 57004 85239
 narrowest.hands.remission

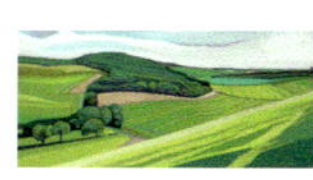

Unhill Woods (2013)
Oil on board, 540 mm × 840 m

View from the Fairmile Track

 SU 57295 83666
 alley.ticket.backs

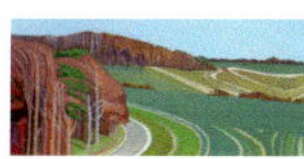

Juniper Hollow (2013)
Oil on board, 765 mm × 940 mm

From an ancient track in Aston Tirrold, looking across at chalk downland on the Berkshire Downs

 SU 54682 83412
 coarser.triathlon.soils

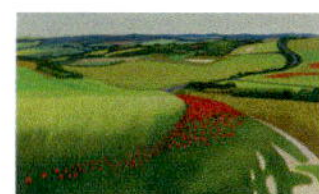

Kingstanding Hill (2012)
Oil on board, 695 mm × 820 mm

 SU 57463 83746
 clarifies.rugs.tribune

 Ordnance Survey National Grid reference
 What Three Words reference

These location references relate to the spot from which the views in the paintings can be seen, rather than location references of the places featured.

Two Rivers Press has been publishing in and about Reading
since 1994. Founded by the artist Peter Hay (1951–2003), the press
continues to delight readers, local and further afield, with its varied list
of individually designed, thought-provoking books.

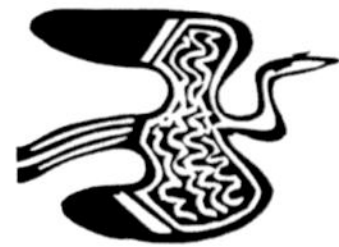